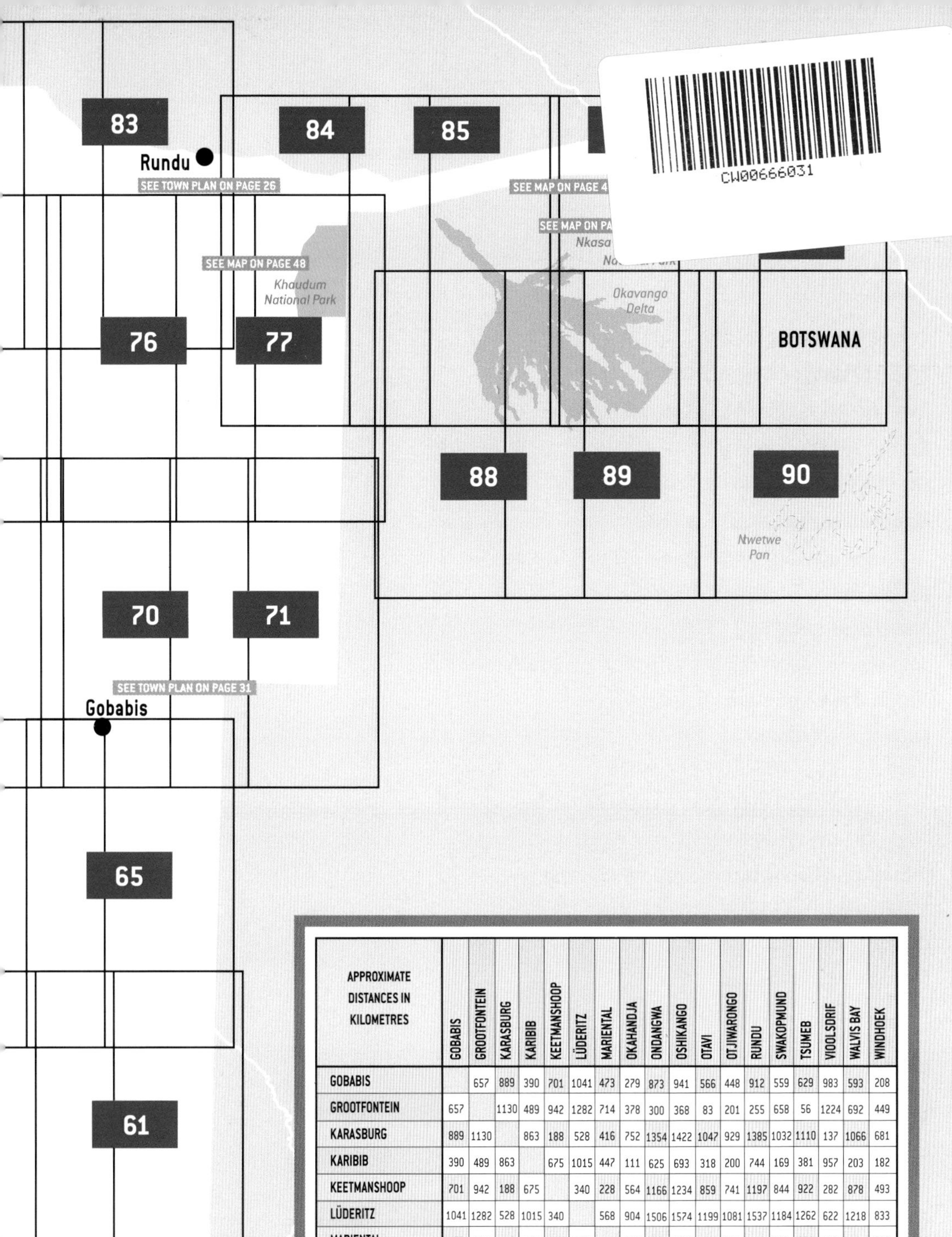

APPROXIMATE DISTANCES IN KILOMETRES	GOBABIS	GROOTFONTEIN	KARASBURG	KARIBIB	KEETMANSHOOP	LÜDERITZ	MARIENTAL	OKAHANDJA	ONDANGWA	OSHIKANGO	OTAVI	OTJIWARONGO	RUNDU	SWAKOPMUND	TSUMEB	VIOOLSDRIF	WALVIS BAY	WINDHOEK
GOBABIS		657	889	390	701	1041	473	279	873	941	566	448	912	559	629	983	593	208
GROOTFONTEIN	657		1130	489	942	1282	714	378	300	368	83	201	255	658	56	1224	692	449
KARASBURG	889	1130		863	188	528	416	752	1354	1422	1047	929	1385	1032	1110	137	1066	681
KARIBIB	390	489	863		675	1015	447	111	625	693	318	200	744	169	381	957	203	182
KEETMANSHOOP	701	942	188	675		340	228	564	1166	1234	859	741	1197	844	922	282	878	493
LÜDERITZ	1041	1282	528	1015	340		568	904	1506	1574	1199	1081	1537	1184	1262	622	1218	833
MARIENTAL	473	714	416	447	228	568		336	938	1006	631	513	969	616	694	510	650	265
OKAHANDJA	279	378	752	111	564	904	336		602	670	295	177	633	280	358	846	314	71
ONDANGWA	873	300	1354	625	1166	1506	938	602		68	118	236	555	794	244	1448	828	673
OSHIKANGO	941	368	1422	693	1234	1574	1006	670	68		186	304	623	862	312	1516	896	741
OTAVI	566	83	1047	318	859	1199	631	295	118	186		118	338	487	63	1141	521	366
OTJIWARONGO	448	201	929	200	741	1081	513	177	236	304	118		456	369	181	1023	403	248
RUNDU	912	255	1385	744	1197	1537	969	633	555	623	338	456		913	311	1479	947	704
SWAKOPMUND	559	658	1032	169	844	1184	616	280	794	862	487	369	913		550	1126	34	351
TSUMEB	629	56	1110	381	922	1262	694	358	244	312	63	181	311	550		1204	584	429
VIOOLSDRIF	983	1224	137	957	282	622	510	846	1448	1516	1141	1023	1479	1126	1204		1160	775
WALVIS BAY	593	692	1066	203	878	1218	650	314	828	896	521	403	947	34	584	1160		385
WINDHOEK	208	449	681	182	493	833	265	71	673	741	366	248	704	351	429	775	385	

Fourth edition published in 2012 by MapStudio™ South Africa

ISBN 978-1-77026-438-0

Production Manager John Loubser
Project Manager Genené Hart
Designers Genené Hart, Nicole Bannister
Cartographer Genené Hart
Researcher Abbygail Greybe
Map Proofreader Nicole Bannister
Reproduction Resolution Colours (Pty) Ltd, Cape Town
Feedback research@mapstudio.co.za
Photo credits © 2012
Jéan du Plessis: All images with the exception of:
Martin Harvey p6(top); 26; 42(top)
Ian Michler p8(bottom)
Images of Africa/Nigel J. Dennis p46
Images of Africa/Peter Pickford p10(bottom)
Wille and Sandra Olivier p28
Printed and bound by Creda Communications
MapStudio™
Unit3, Block B, M5 Park, Eastman Road, Maitland, 7405
PO Box 193, Maitland, 7404
Tel: 0860 10 50 50, www.mapstudio.co.za

NAMIBIA

Contents

Introduction

Namibia, land of shifting sand, is a rough diamond on the African coast waiting to be cut and polished by any eager travellers making their way through this vast land. The treacherous Skeleton Coast lures you in, while Sossusvlei's giant waves of red sand mystify you, along with the numerous ghost towns (the social scrapyards of past glories in the world of diamond mining), drawing you ever closer with the promise of stories untold. There's wildlife in abundance and some of the natural world's most breath-taking landscapes, dramatic vistas and awe-inspiring caves to explore, although the Fish River Canyon must take pride of place as one of the world's great natural wonders. Some of the most desired national parks on the continent beckon the traveller, who'll usually be welcomed with open arms by the sub-2-million population who inhabit this ancient land, among them the legendary San who still sail barefoot across Namibia's great seas of sand. People come to Namibia to lose themselves yet, lost in all this space, many instead succeed only in finding themselves.

'If your mouth turns into a knife, it will cut off your lips.'
'The trees never meet [but people do].' – Namibian proverbs.

History

A LONG, LONG TIME AGO ...

Evidence of Stone Age occupation of Namibia exists in rock paintings estimated to be 25,000 years or older. Centuries later various groups of San hunter-gatherers wandered in and settled parts of this vast expanse of land, and later Khoi [the ancestors of the Nama], Bantu-speaking tribes, Hereros, Basters and Owambos made their home in Namibia.

TAKE ME TO YOUR LEADER

Namibia's long history is of human courage, African tribal migration, settlement and conflict, a position as a strategic military stronghold along the African coastline, colonial exploration and exploitation by Britain, Germany and South Africa. UN-supervised elections were held in November 1989 and Namibia became independent on 21 March 1990. Independence and a period of blissful co-existence brought every promise for a bright future, despite some minor political instability and sporadic acts of violence.

Almost four times the size of Great Britain, Namibia is one of Africa's most sparsely populated countries, largely owing to the arid nature of this low-rainfall area.

COMINGS AND GOINGS

The 1480s were a busy time along Namibia's coast as first Diego Cão [a Portuguese navigator] planted a stone cross [*padrão*] at Cape Cross in 1486 [roughly 130km north of Swakopmund], followed two years later by Bartolomeu Dias at present-day Lüderitz [then Angra Pequena, or Little Bay]. The spot where Dias erected his cross was appropriately named Dias Point. Considering the proliferation of British, German and Portuguese influences on Southern Africa, it's ironic that a Swedish adventurer and explorer [named Charles John Andersson] should coin the name South West Africa in his travel journal, a name which stuck, albeit with the somewhat temporary adjustment to German South West Africa when Otto von Bismarck proclaimed the country a German protectorate in 1884.

Cormorants nesting on a wrecked ship on the treacherous Skeleton Coast. Many a ship has run aground on this bitter coastline.

Neighbouring South Africa sent forces in to overthrow the Germans during World War I, and thus brought the territory under their administration after the War. In 1966 SWAPO [the South West African People's Organisation] took up arms against the occupying forces of their 'rulers', and after much fighting and many years of strife, free and fair elections were arranged following the implementation of United Nations Resolution 435 in 1989. SWAPO won at the polls that same year, thus signalling independence for the land after more than a century of foreign rule. Long-time advocate for independence, Dr Sam Nujoma, became his country's first president, and remained in office till 2005 when he was succeeded by Hifikepunye Pohamba.

San rock paintings at Twyfelfontein.

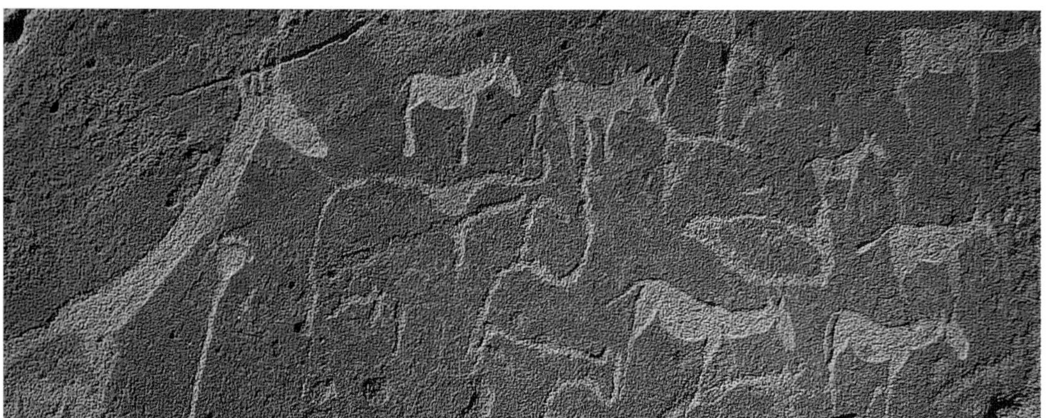

'The earth is not ours, it is a treasure we hold in trust for future generations.'
Old African proverb.

History

DIVIDE AND RULE
After independence Namibia was divided into 13 regions: the north comprised Omusati, Oshana, Ohangwena and Oshikoto; the Kunene lies in the northwest; Kavango and Caprivi in the northeast; the central part is made up of Erongo, Otjozondjupa, Omaheke, Khomas and Hardap; and, finally, there is Karas in the south.

Namibia's democratic constitution is highly regarded by the international community, and the country is ruled by a multiparty parliament, with the overriding policy of national reconciliation and unity striving to embrace the noble concepts of tolerance and respect for differing political views, as well as racial and ethnic harmony. Power is divided between the executive, the legislature and the judiciary under the constitution.

THE ART OF DIPLOMACY
Namibia hosts the following diplomatic missions: Algeria, Angola, Botswana, Brazil, China, Congo, Cuba, Egypt, the European Union, Finland, France, Germany, Ghana, India, Indonesia, Italy, Kenya, Libya, Malawi, Malaysia, Mexico, the Netherlands, Nigeria, Portugal, the Russian Federation, South Africa, Spain, Sweden, Great Britain and Ireland, the United States of America, Venezuela, Zambia and Zimbabwe.

LANGUAGES
English is the official language, but with numerous different tribes as well as colonial influences, it's hardly surprising to find a multitude of languages spoken throughout Namibia. Bantu languages are spoken by the Owambo, Herero, Kavango, Caprivians and Tswana; the descendants of colonial explorers and masters speak one or more of Afrikaans, German and English (although many Namibians can communicate in one or more of these three languages); and Khoisan languages are spoken by the San, Nama and Damara people.

POPULATION
Based on figures from the official 2001 census, Namibia's population swelled by over 400,000 people during the previous decade, reaching a high of more than 2,100,000 people. Interestingly, there are 50,000 more women than men. The most densely populated region is the Khomas (which includes Windhoek), with over a quarter of a million people, little more than 100 'head' ahead of Ohangwena. The Kavango region occupies third spot, lagging 50,000 'heads' behind. Unfortunately, it's not a good country for individuals who suffer from agoraphobia (fear of open spaces), as Namibia enjoys one of the world's lowest population densities – on average there are less than two people per square kilometre.

Namibia's ghost towns offer a window back into the country's diamond mining boom days. Bogenfels (top) and Kolmanskop (left) are both popular tourist attractions.

Namibians work in many different fields, ranging from the hunter-gatherers to formal farmers, in addition to a highly skilled and diverse urban population.

People

Himba women boast refined features, elaborate hairstyles and traditional adornments.

Namibia's hunter-gatherer SAN are around 35,000 strong in numbers and enjoy a proud tradition as great story-tellers, musicians, mimics and dancers. Their forefathers wandered South Africa's plains for thousands of years, leaving a wealth of rock art and engravings (notably the White Lady painting found in the Brandberg, as well as Twyfelfontein, the San's equivalent of the Louvre) to stake their claim as one of Namibia's oldest peoples. Some of their paintings date back almost 30,000 years. A large proportion of the San now live a 'normal' life in villages, while some continue to enjoy a traditional, nomadic existence (mostly in Botswana).

THE CAPRIVIANS number around 80,000 and live in the Caprivi Strip. They are mostly subsistence farmers who make their living from cultivating crops, keeping cattle and fishing. These resourceful people are adaptable to the seasons: those living on the eastern flood plains of the Zambezi and Chobe rivers move seasonally, depending on the level of the floods.

Namibia's COLOURED community, along with the Basters, hails from the Cape Province in South Africa: both speak Afrikaans as their home language, although with different accents and dialects. Many are fishermen who ply the waters around Walvis Bay for their livelihood, while there are a large number of well-educated coloureds, many of whom enjoy professional employment.

THE DAMARA are proud to be one of the country's oldest cultural groups, and from their ranks come many politicians who are among the most eloquent in Namibia's parliament. Their traditional homeland, Damaraland, was renamed the Erongo Region after independence in 1990, with a population numbering over 100,000.

THE HERERO migrated to Namibia centuries ago. They suffered great population losses during the colonial wars and in the 1904/5 Herero Uprising. Pastoral cattle breeders, they have retained their bonds of family life and tribal solidarity despite the wartime losses and proudly celebrate their national consciousness with a festival on Maherero Day in Okahandja every August, which includes a display of military pomp through the town's streets.

THE HIMBA are a semi-nomadic tribe of pastoralists based in the Kunene region. They live in cone-shaped 'homes' made from saplings, palm leaves, mud and dung. Proud yet friendly, these famously beautiful people are tall, slender and statuesque. They adorn themselves with bracelets, anklets, necklaces, iron belts and beautiful beads made from shells. The women protect their skin from the harsh desert sun by coating their bodies with red ochre and fat.

The Kavango River provides a lifeline for THE KAVANGO people, whose numbers have swelled to over 200,000, causing 'domestic overcrowding': on average, six and a half people live in each household! Many of the younger generation are migratory farm labourers, miners and urban workers, while those who remain closer to home

Herero women wear distinctive Victorian-style dresses and interesting headwear.

Great storytellers and poets, the Namas of the southern region find their language on the list of 'Languages in Danger of Disappearing'.

ply the Kavango for fish, cultivate crops on the surrounding fertile plains or tend their cattle.

THE NAMA are Namibia's only pure Khoi descendants. Certain distinctive characteristics, such as the women's small and slender hands and feet, make the Khoi easily distinguishable. Nama have a natural talent for music, poetry and prose. An example of a traditional dance is the well-known Nama 'stap'. Numerous proverbs, riddles, tales and poems have been handed down orally from generation to generation. Nama women are highly skilled in sewing. Their embroidery and appliqué work, today regarded as a traditional art form, consist of brightly coloured motifs inspired by their rural environment and lifestyles. The content of their work is often expressive and humorous, as seen in the colourful, traditional patchwork dresses that the Nama women wear.

OWAMBO is a collective name for a number of tribes living in central northern Namibia and southern Angola. Of the nine Owambo tribes, the Kwanyama group is the largest. The most striking feature of the traditional Owambo social system is the predominance of matrilineal descent, which determines the laws of inheritance and succession, as well as post-marital residency. As a result of external factors such as the Christian doctrine, migrant labour and economic independence, there has been a distinct shift towards a patrilineally organised society.

THE REHOBOTH BASTERS can trace their roots back to the day Jan van Riebeeck's settlers first set foot at the Cape of Good Hope in South Africa. The children that resulted from the meetings of the European settlers and the Khoi were branded 'Coloureds' or 'Bastards'. In 1868 almost 100 Baster families migrated to Namibia, ultimately putting down roots at the hot-water springs called Rehoboth. Today the Baster community consists of approximately 72,000 people. Their mother tongue is Afrikaans and, at their own request, they have been registered as Rehoboth Basters. The Basters regard themselves as a separate community from the Coloureds by virtue of their unique history and the fact that they have been living in their own territory for more than a century.

THE TOPNAARS are a hardy people of Nama origin who have lived on the banks of the Kuiseb River for many years. Belonging to the Khoi people, they speak the Nama language with its guttural clicks and high musical pitch. Central to their culinary tradition is the *!nara* melon, a large and nutritious fruit which is endemic to the Namib. The *!nara* melon is believed to enjoy certain medicinal properties.

An elderly Nama man in Keetmanshoop enjoying his pipe, perhaps while trying to solve one of the many age-old Nama riddles.

THE TSWANA are Namibia's smallest cultural group, numbering around a mere 8000. Namibia's rural Tswana live in The Corridor, a narrow strip along the border with Botswana, where they are involved in cattle farming. Many of them have bought commercial farms in the Gobabis district.

THE WHITES (descended from European stock and almost all urban-dwellers and farmers) number around 100,000 of Namibia's population, and the majority are Afrikaans-speaking, with German and English speakers making up the rest. Roughly 150 Portuguese families (originally from Angola) still call Namibia home.

Kids in the Caprivi area take a moment to smile for the camera, despite the pain of a broken arm.

'It never rains, but it pours' seems to sum up Namibia's unreliable rainfall patterns over much of the country for much of the year.

Nature

The Greater Kestrel is able to hover in the air as it watches the ground beneath it for prey.

THE SIZE OF IT

Namibia covers an area of almost 825,000km², in parts as wide as 1440km and in others as narrow as 350km. You'd need more than 5700km of measuring tape to accurately measure its perimeter; over 1500km is coastline (from the mouth of the Kunene down to the Orange River mouth). Namibia also controls an exclusive economic zone of some 200 nautical miles off its coast, which amounts to well over half a million square kilometres of ocean.

QUITE A RELIEF

A large portion of Namibia consists of a wide open plateau that spills into neighbouring countries at altitudes of between 900m and 1300m. In parts massive escarpments jut up from around the coast; the incisions were created over centuries by geological processes as well as the effects of erosion caused by vast river systems, for example in the Fish River Canyon. Aside from becoming president, the highest point a Namibian can reach is by climbing the 2579m high Brandberg ('burnt mountain'). Namibia offers geologists endless pleasures, not least because so many of its spectacular rock formations are so beautifully exposed. Notable among these are the granite hills of the Spitzkoppe, which are remnants of great masses of magma that were forced into the earth's crust around 130 million years ago when the Gondwana supercontinent started breaking up to separate Namibia from South America.

Elephants enjoying a drink at a local water hole.

BEAUTIFUL BIRDS

Well over 600 species of bird have been recorded (11 endemic), with around 500 breeding in Namibia. Notable endemic species include the Herero Chat, Monteiro's Hornbill, Damara Tern, Rockrunner, Long-toed Plover and the Greater Swamp Warbler. The majestic African Fish Eagle is found near water (as well as on the country's coat of arms), while the Sociable Weaver will enchant bird-watchers with its amazing system of communal

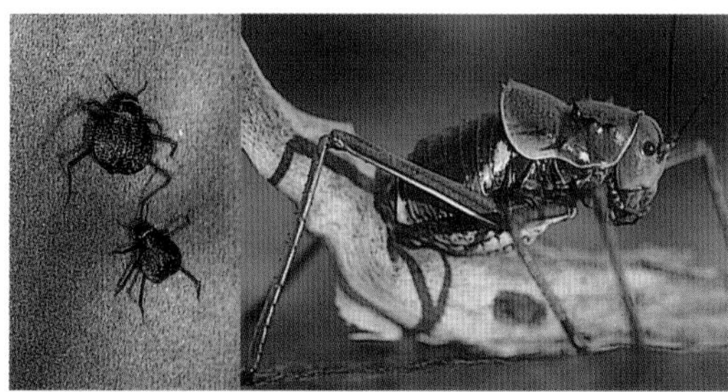

Above left: Two beetles scurry along the desert sand.
Above right: An armoured ground cricket.

nests – which it constructs in trees or on telephone poles – that can house hundreds of birds (some nests have survived for many decades). The brightly coloured Malachite Kingfisher, with its short tail and relatively long, red beak, is one of hundreds of species that grace the waters of the Caprivi region.

AN ABUNDANCE OF WILDLIFE

Namibia enjoys a glorious wildlife population, with numerous species of game throughout the country, including eight endemic species of mammal (among them the black-faced impala, various mice, gerbils and bats). The big game includes leopard, lion and cheetah, in addition to elephant, rhino (white and black), hippopotamus and giraffe, as well as buffalo, Burchell's zebra and Hartmann's mountain zebra. The numerous species of antelope include eland, the greater kudu, roan and sable antelope, gemsbok, wildebeest, waterbuck, lechwe, sitatunga, red hartbeest, nyala, springbok, impala, reedbuck, oribi, bushbuck and the 5kg Damara dik-dik, which only stands up to 40cm high on its stick-like legs. Jackals, hyena, wild dogs and warthogs will also put in an appearance on many a wildlife expedition, as well as dassies (rock hyrax), chacma baboons and vervet monkeys. The harsh landscape naturally limits the variety and abundance of wildlife to some extent, yet equally it provides the perfect survival conditions for a number of endemic animals. The Namib desert boasts a wide range of toktokkies (tenebrionids) and other beetles (such as the 'fog-trapping' beetle), as well as lizards (Skoog's lizard burrows to safety in the sand with a unique corkscrew motion) and a wide range of other interesting insects and reptiles.

The welwitschia is an ancient plant of the Namib region that can live for more than a thousand years – yet in all that time it will produce only two leaves.

HARD-HEADED FLORA

Namibia's dramatically different climates (from the coast to the harsh interior) create an environment that caters for a wide range of plant life, although the land is best known for its hardier species which have overcome the elements to thrive. Most famous is probably the endemic welwitschia of the Namib Desert, which can live from 500 to 2000 years, one of the oldest known plants in the world. There are more than 120 tree species, including the umbrella-shaped camel-thorn, the baobab, quiver trees (or kokerboom), marula, paper bark trees, mopane, figs, leadwood, jackalsbessie, Boesmangif (Bushman's poison) and Makalani palms. Other plant life includes reeds and palms on the flood plains and the common driedoring flower (three-thorned flower). A fascinating array of lichens (there are more than 100 kinds throughout Namibia, some of which are endemic) can be found in the desert – these rely totally on moisture from the coastal fog for their survival. In all,

Flowering lithops.

Namibia has more than 200 endemic plant species, including the lithops (commonly known as the flowering stones). Other well-known plants include the halfmens, the elephant's foot and a number of dwarf succulents which are found near Lüderitz.

The San once used the unusual hollow branches of the quiver tree (kokerboom) as quivers to hold their arrows.

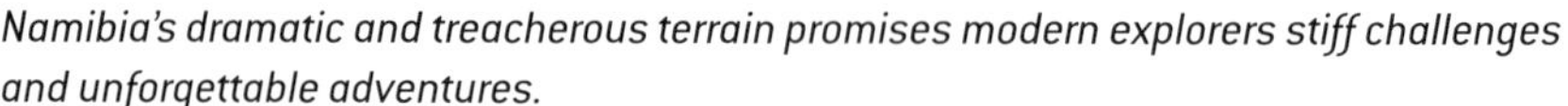

Namibia's dramatic and treacherous terrain promises modern explorers stiff challenges and unforgettable adventures.

Activities

SAND'S UP

Namibia's coastal dunes provide endless enjoyment for visitors, and are one of the best places in the world to enjoy sand-skiing and sand-boarding – the idea is to push off the top of a dune and lie on the board as it slides down. Speeds easily reach 70kph. Dune-boarding may seem more refined, but it requires more skill to stand up on a small surfboard as it shoots down the side of a dune. Quad biking involves riding 4-wheel motorcycles over and around the dunes. Though these organised trips are well regulated, the reckless use of quad bikes is increasingly damaging the fragile environment, and harming the coastal wildlife.

SADDLE UP

Namibia has perfect conditions for horse riding, with routes crossing mountains, bush and wooded areas to desert plains and dunes. Alternatively, for a more Arabian experience, camel riding is available in places along the coast. For something completely different, and authentically Namibian, try an exciting donkey-cart drive, the traditional transport of the Topnaar people.

TAKE THE PLUNGE

Adding an exhilarating dimension to a visit to the Namib desert is a trip in a hot-air balloon. For those who enjoy taking their lives into their own hands and having adrenaline pumping through their veins, skydiving over land and sea is the answer. Paragliding enthusiasts occasionally undertake powered paragliding excursions along the coast.

Quad biking on Namibia's dunes is an increasingly popular pursuit and there are outlets between Swakopmund and Walvis Bay.

Top: 4x4 trips through the desert sands might seem like a ticket to ride wild, but respect for the environment and caution for your personal safety should be uppermost in your mind.
Above: Desert hikes are one of the ultimate human tests against the elements.

OVER WATER

White-water canoeing has taken off in a big way on the Kunene River, but it's advisable to join a tour offered by an experienced adventure company if you're not experienced. Between Ruacana and Epupa there are rapids at Ondorusu and Enyandi, while Epupa Falls is set in scenic surroundings and is blessed with interesting vegetation and bird life. Canoeing safaris are offered down the Orange River, departing from Noordoewer or Aussenkehr and ending at Aussenkehr or the Fish River mouth respectively.

UNDER WATER

Dragon's Breath Cave (on Harasib farm) lays claim to the world's largest known subterranean lake. To explore it you will need valid cave-diving qualifications and gear and more courage than the average person. Harasib Cave and Lake are reached through an opening found on Ghaub Mountain, and both are worth exploring. The lake has an amazing natural display of stalactites and stalagmites. Lying 24km away from Tsumeb is the 76m deep

Namibia offers a wide range of activities, from sedate family trips to high-adrenaline, blood-curdling adventures requiring great skill and courage.

Lake Otjikoto (also only for qualified divers) which will yield a treasure trove of abandoned weapons and armaments dumped here after World War I: great wreck diving for the experienced diver. On the whole, Namibia's coast presents tough conditions for scuba divers, with visibility ranging from half a metre up to usually no more than four metres. To add to the visual difficulty, temperatures in these waters range from 9°C to 17°C.

CASTING YOUR LINE

Aspects that make coastal angling from the beach especially enjoyable are the peaceful desert environment and the uncrowded beaches. Namibia's dams in the interior offer several options for those wishing to try their hand at freshwater angling. The far eastern tip of the Caprivi, at the confluence of the Chobe and Zambezi rivers, is regarded as a tiger-fishing paradise second to none.

Sunset fishing on an uncrowded beach, with the desert sands behind you, will help clear the mental cobwebs from most city slickers' heads.

HUNTING

Namibia's abundant wildlife attracts hunting enthusiasts from afar to partake in trophy and safari hunting, bird hunting, as well as the ancient art of bow hunting. Written permission must be obtained from the farmer whose land your hunting party intends using before the authorities will issue a hunting permit. Note that the official term 'huntable game' strictly excludes any protected animals.

FOUR-WHEEL DRIVING

There are countless four-wheel driving opportunities in this sandy and rocky landscape, both supervised and unsupervised. Some of the more popular and challenging include: the Dorsland Trek 4x4 Route, Isabis 4x4 Trail, Saddle Hill, Topnaar 4x4 Trail, Conception Bay Route and the Naukluft Route.

TAKE A HIKE

Owing to high summer temperatures, tough terrain and scarcity of water, hiking in Namibia requires careful planning. Hiking is not advisable in the summer months when temperatures often exceed 40 °C. Some of the best destinations and trails include: the Fish River Canyon (one of Southern Africa's top five), the Naukluft Hiking Trail, the Ugab River Hiking Trail (in the south of the Skeleton Coast Park), the Dassie Trails Network, the Sweet Thorn Hiking Trail, the Tok Tokkie Trails, the Waterberg Hiking Trail and the Waterberg Wilderness Trail.

MOUNTAINEERING AND ROCK CLIMBING

Spitzkoppe's vast granite dome rises about 700m above the desert plains between Windhoek and Swakopmund. Also referred to as Namibia's Matterhorn, the Spitzkoppe – with its almost perpendicular slopes – is one of the great mountaineering opportunities in Africa. Brandberg is a sought-after area for both mountaineers and backpackers. Due to the extremely rugged terrain and limited water, excursions should only be undertaken by experienced and fit backpackers. Abseiling is also gaining popularity due to some of Namibia's spectacular rock formations.

Hot-air balloon rides offer visitors spectacular views of the Namibian landscape.

Towns

Towns

Most travel guides promise that Namibia's towns (especially the 'small little holes in the ground' out in the middle of nowhere) are good merely for stopping, stretching and stocking up on petrol and some niceties. Of course, it all depends how you look at it and what you're looking for! You won't find the CRASH-BOOM-BANG sights and sounds that draw the horrible hordes to the junk-food destinations. Thank your lucky stars: that's not what makes Namibia unique. The towns speak of a heritage shared across cultures and oceans, and there's no rush here: nothing is going to dash off before you get to it. If you tune into Namibia's frequency her beauty will go bang-crash-boom in tiny ripples through your soul. Drift. Wander around small museums in tiny towns. Take 10 minutes to look at the quaint memorials to bygone heroes. Ask the locals about the weather, and the best place to make a braai. This is not an 'instant' holiday spot, it's an adventure waiting to be lived.

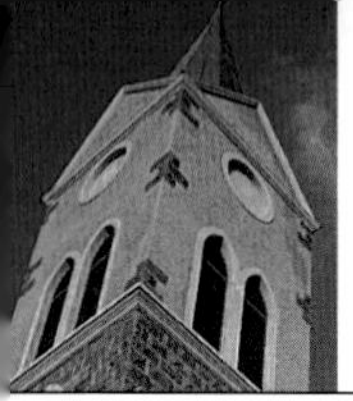

Namibia's capital is a modern, vibrant African city whose high-rises and pedestrian shopping malls speak of prosperity and progress.

Windhoek

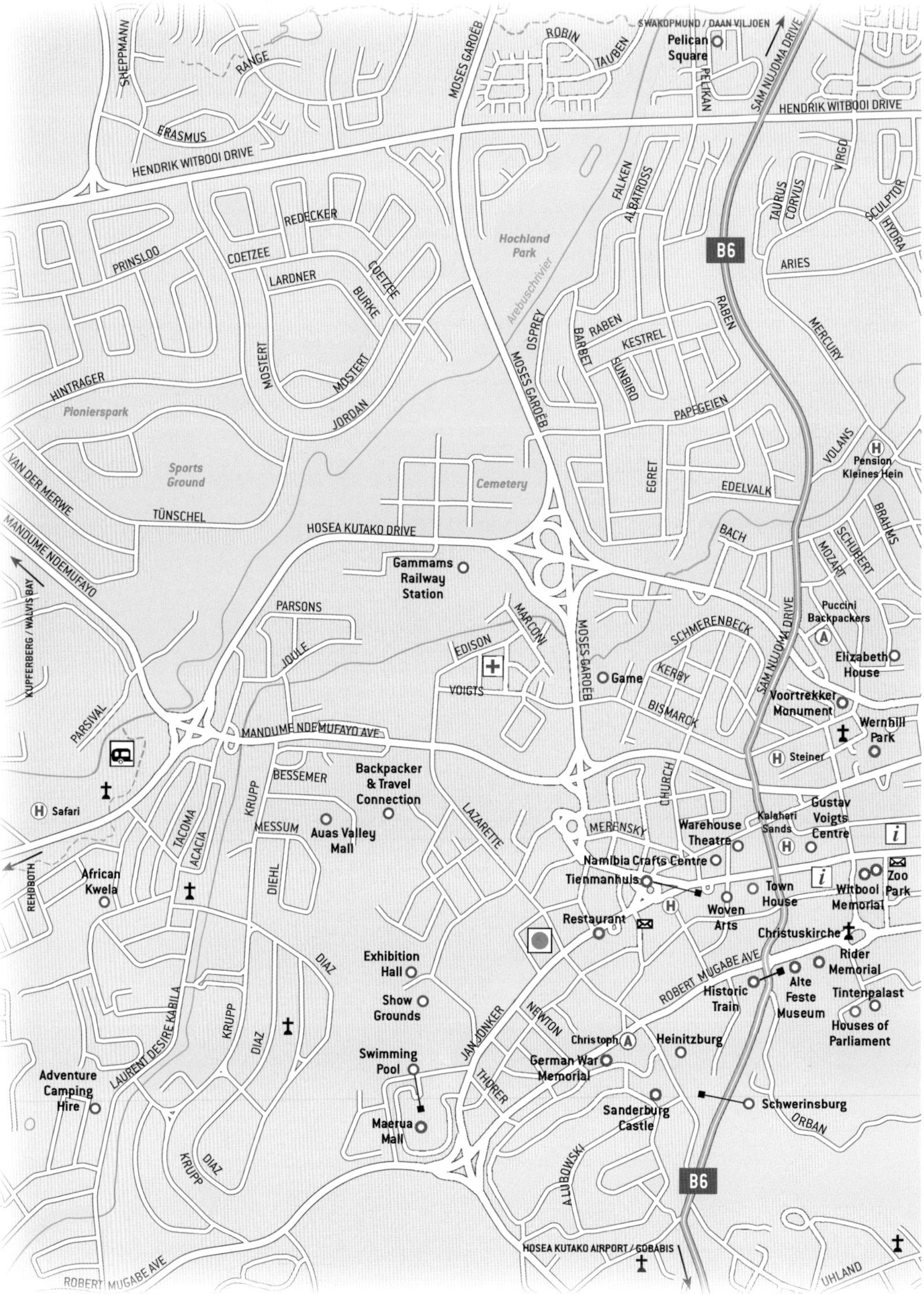
SWAKOPMUND / DAAN VILJOEN
Pelican Square
SHEPPMANN
RANGE
ROBIN
TAUBEN
PELIKAN
MOSES GAROËB
SAM NUJOMA DRIVE
HENDRIK WITBOOI DRIVE
ERASMUS
HENDRIK WITBOOI DRIVE
VIRGO
TAURUS
CORVUS
SCULPTOR
HYDRA
FALKEN
ALBATROSS
REDECKER
COETZEE
PRINSLOO
LARDNER
COETZEE
BURKE
Hochland Park
Arebuschrivier
B6
ARIES
MERCURY
RABEN
RABEN
KESTREL
BARBET
SUNBIRD
OSPREY
MOSES GAROËB
MOSTERT
MOSTERT
JORDAN
HINTRAGER
Pionierspark
PAPEGEIEN
VOLANS
Pension Kleines Hein
Sports Ground
Cemetery
EGRET
EDELVALK
BRAHMS
VAN DER MERWE
TÜNSCHEL
HOSEA KUTAKO DRIVE
BACH
SCHUBERT
MOZART
MANDUME NDEMUFAYO
Gammams Railway Station
KUPFERBERG / WALVIS BAY
PARSONS
MARCONI
MOSES GAROËB
SCHMERENBECK
SAM NUJOMA DRIVE
Puccini Backpackers
JOULE
EDISON
VOIGTS
Game
KERBY
Elizabeth House
BISMARCK
Voortrekker Monument
Wernhill Park
PARSIVAL
MANDUME NDEMUFAYO AVE
Steiner
BESSEMER
Backpacker & Travel Connection
CHURCH
KRUPP
Gustav Voigts Centre
Safari
MESSUM
Auas Valley Mall
LAZARETTE
MERENSKY
Warehouse Theatre
Kalahari Sands
TACOMA
ACACIA
Namibia Crafts Centre
Tienmanhuis
Town House
Zoo Park
REHOBOTH
African Kwela
DIEHL
Witbool Memorial
Woven Arts
Restaurant
Christuskirche
Exhibition Hall
DIAZ
ROBERT MUGABE AVE
Rider Memorial
Alte Feste Museum
Historic Train
Tintenpalast
Show Grounds
NEWTON
Houses of Parliament
LAURENT DESIRE KABILA
KRUPP
DIAZ
JAN JONKER
Christoph
Heinitzburg
Adventure Camping Hire
Swimming Pool
German War Memorial
THORER
Sanderburg Castle
Schwerinsburg
ORBAN
Maerua Mall
KRUPP
DIAZ
ALUBOWSKI
B6
HOSEA KUTAKO AIRPORT / GOBABIS
ROBERT MUGABE AVE
UHLAND

Located 1500m above sea level, Windhoek sits sheltered by the Eros Mountains (slightly north) and the Aus Mountains (south of the capital).

Windhoek

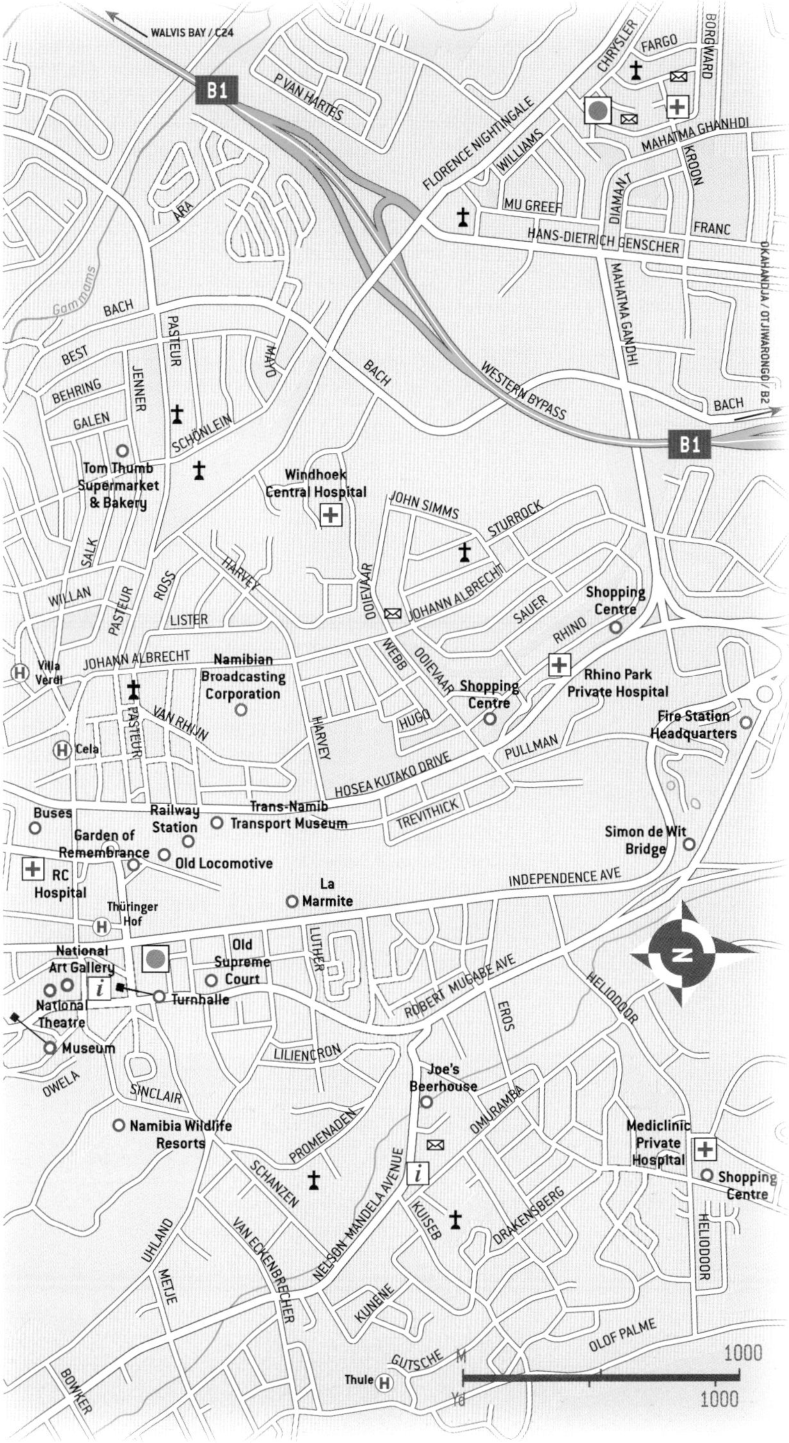

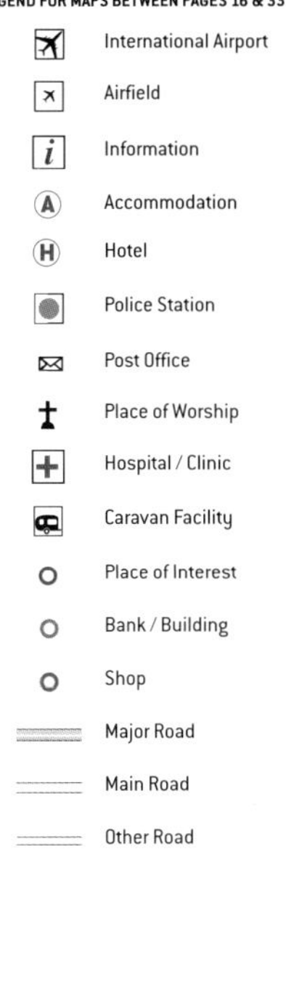

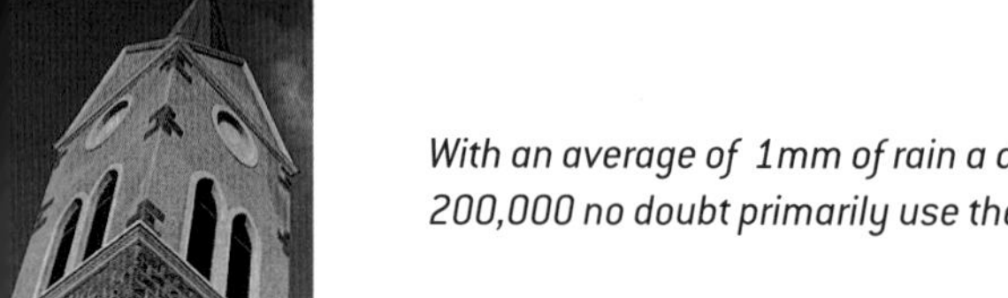

With an average of 1mm of rain a day, Windhoek's population of just over 200,000 no doubt primarily use their umbrellas for sun protection.

Windhoek

Relaxed, yet alive with people and an array of vibrant cultures, Windhoek gives visitors a generous feeling of welcome without engulfing them like a typical western capital. Despite its large proportion of indigenous inhabitants, the concrete face of Windhoek is very German in nature, the architecture and numerous war memorials paying homage to the former colonial masters.

Windhoek has a reasonable entertainment infrastructure, with well-attended and popular nightclubs, bars and restaurants. For visitors or locals seeking engagements of a more cerebral nature, there are art galleries and museums that boast impressive exhibits, as well as a theatre and a cinema (with five screens). If you're architecturally inclined you'll be able to amuse yourself for hours in Windhoek, which boasts a rich tradition of colonial German buildings in addition to newer post-modernist constructions. And, of course, the three castles on the hills (all completed by 1917) overlooking the city centre provide further fascination. Heinitzburg, the second to be built, is now an up-market hotel and a good spot for sundowners.

WHERE THE STREETS HAVE FAMOUS NAMES

A walk down Independence Avenue will offer views of some stunning German colonial architecture, the Clock Tower, Zoo Park's lawns and palm trees, the Curt von François statue, and the Augustino Neto Gardens. You'll also notice some famous road names: Sam Nujoma Drive, Robert Mugabe Avenue and Nelson Mandela Drive.

THE RIDER MEMORIAL

An enormous statue stands at the entrance to the Alte Feste (Old Fort), Windhoek's oldest surviving building, and now the National Museum of Namibia. The statue – *Reiter Denkmal* (the Rider Memorial) – depicts a larger-than-life but typical German Protection Force soldier. The statue was erected in memory of the Schutztruppe (German soldiers) who died during the 1903–07 wars against the Herero and Nama.

LOOK AT THIS

Post Street Mall boasts the largest display of meteorites in the world – or so say the locals – of which 33 make up a sculpture in the middle of the Mall! The Gibeon meteorites rained down on earth probably 600 million years ago, over 20 tons of rock (77 meteorites in all) having been collected in the area around Gibeon, near Mariental.

The Rider Memorial.

In 1959 Windhoek's black population was forcibly removed to Katutura, which is Herero for 'we have no dwelling place'.

Windhoek

ALOE-ALOE

The aloe – a hardy plant with large, fleshy leaves for storing water in arid conditions – is an icon of Namibia. Aloes usually present themselves in a stunning winter display around town, but they can also be appreciated in the Windhoek Botanical Gardens.

DAAN VILJOEN GAME PARK

Close to Windhoek, Daan Viljoen Game Park is equipped for travellers and offers driving opportunities for standard cars. The park has three main trails: Wag-'n-Bietjie (Buffalo-thorn) Trail, Rooibos (Bushwillow) Trail and Sweet-thorn Trail. It offers good game spotting and has a prolific bird life (including the Damara Rockjumper and the Rosy-faced Lovebird). Walking is relatively safe as four of the Big (and dangerous) Five don't inhabit the Park (lion, elephant, rhino and buffalo).

> ***Top Tip***
> *For hikers, the purchase of* Birds of Daan Viljoen *(from the parks office) will be money well spent: it has a check list of bird species as well as other useful information on the birds and the park.*

Christuskirche, Windhoek's Evangelical Lutheran church, consecrated in 1910.

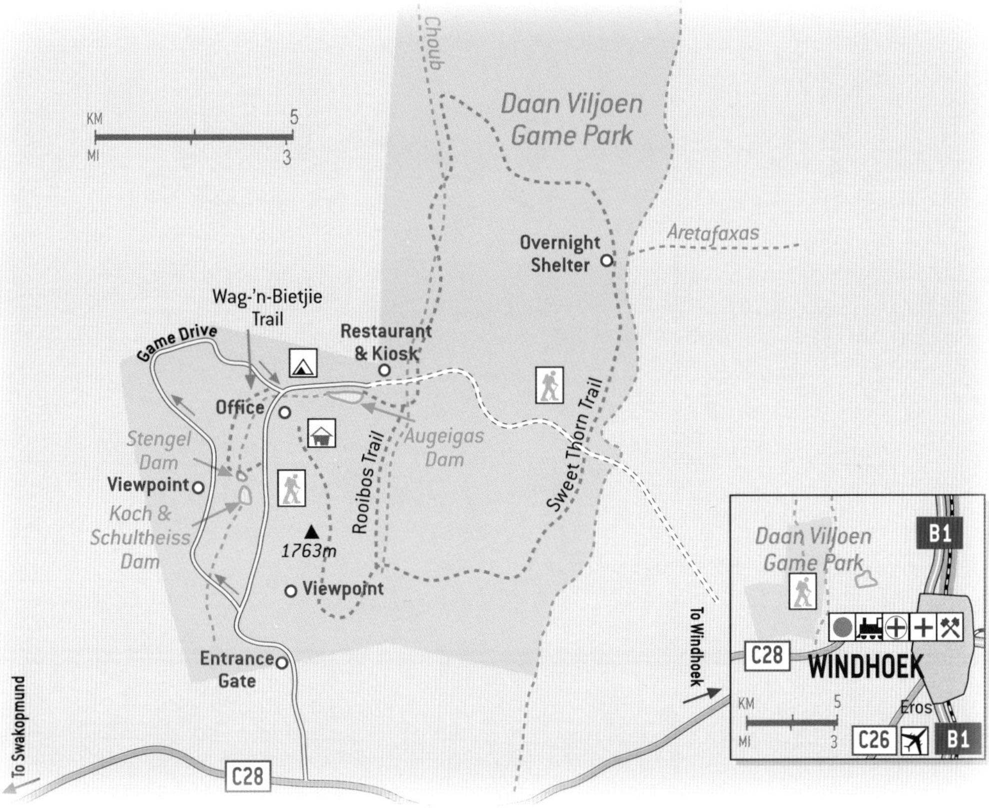

Daan Viljoen Game Park
Choub
KM 5
MI 3
Overnight Shelter
Aretafaxas
Wag-'n-Bietjie Trail
Game Drive
Restaurant & Kiosk
Office
Stengel Dam
Augeigas Dam
Rooibos Trail
Sweet Thorn Trail
Viewpoint
Koch & Schultheiss Dam
1763m
Viewpoint
Entrance Gate
To Swakopmund
C28
To Windhoek
Daan Viljoen Game Park
B1
C28
WINDHOEK
Eros
KM 5
MI 3
C26
B1

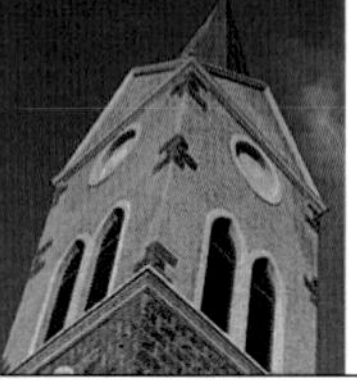

Namibia's holiday mecca, Swakop (as the locals call it) offers lovely beaches for anglers, surfers, bathers and sun-worshippers to share.

Swakopmund

Swakop is small enough to be explored on foot, and interesting enough to make the effort worthwhile. It's also the adventure and activity centre of Nambia (which includes parachuting, sand-boarding and dune-bike riding) and as such it's no surprise that the town is extremely tourist friendly, while maintaining the ability to slip back into sleepy-hollow mode at certain times of the week, month or year. There are plenty of cultural attractions (libraries, museums, commercial art galleries, curio stores and interesting buildings) to occupy the non-adrenaline junkie.

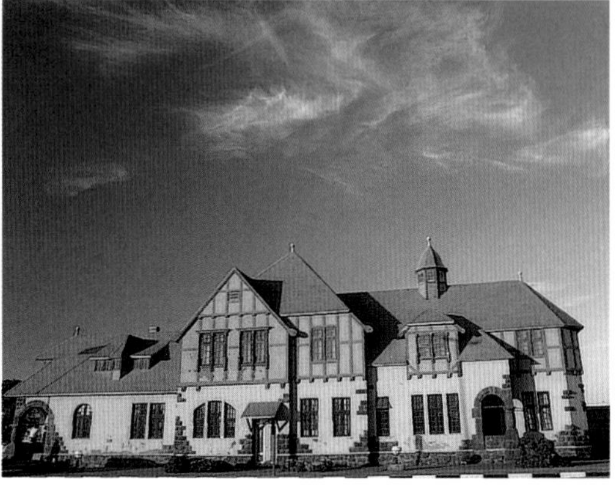

Swakopmund Prison, often mistaken by visitors for a hotel.

> **Top Tip**
> *The Sam Cohen Library has 7000 volumes of Africana books and literature on Swakopmund, as well as old photos, maps and German and English newspapers dating back to 1898.*

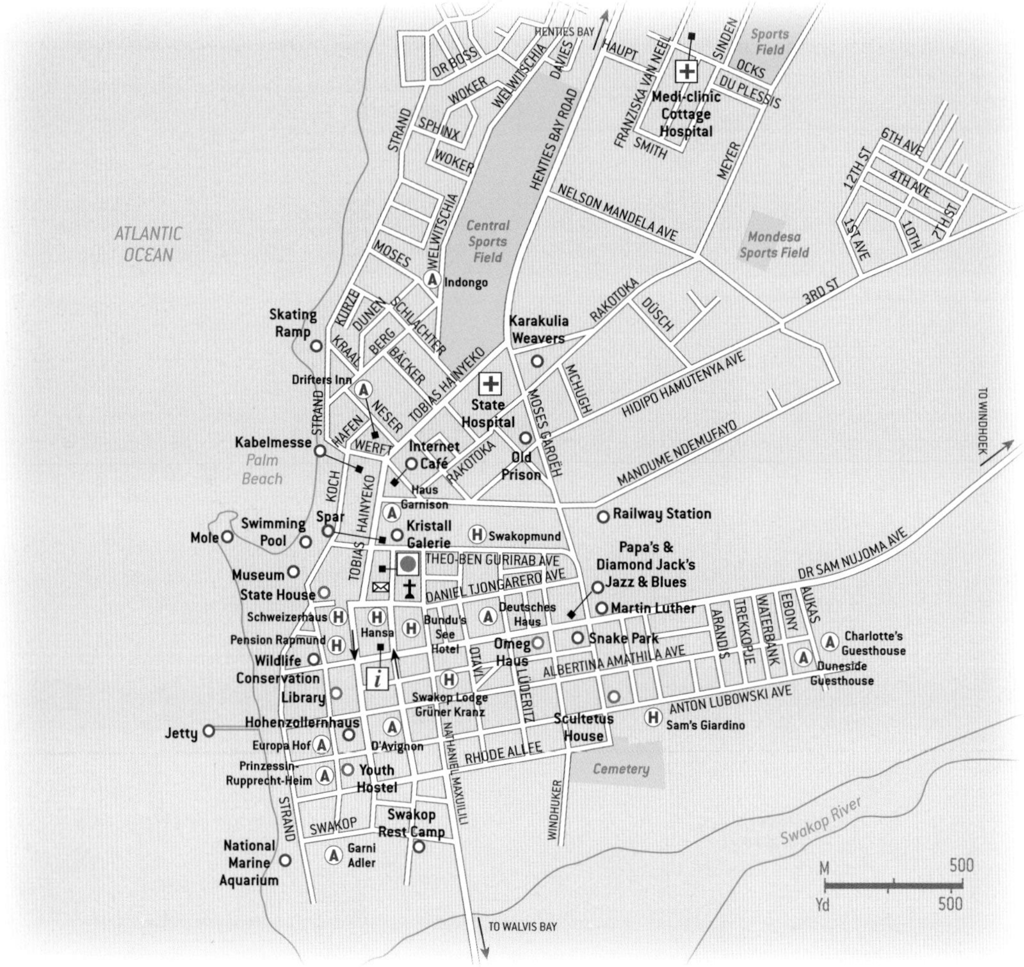

HENTIES BAY
DR BOSS
WOKER
WELWITSCHIA
DAVIES
HAUPT
FRANZISKA VAN NEEL
SINDEN
Sports Field
OCKS
DU PLESSIS
Medi-clinic Cottage Hospital
SMITH
STRAND
SPHINX
HENTIES BAY ROAD
MEYER
6TH AVE
12TH ST
4TH AVE
NELSON MANDELA AVE
1ST AVE
10TH
7TH ST
ATLANTIC OCEAN
Central Sports Field
MOSES
Mondesa Sports Field
Indongo
RAKOTOKA
DÜSCH
3RD ST
Skating Ramp
KURZE
DÜNEN
SCHLACHTER
KRAAL
BERG
Karakulia Weavers
BÄCKER
TOBIAS HAINYEKO
MCHUGH
HIDIPO HAMUTENYA AVE
Drifters Inn
NESER
State Hospital
MOSES GARÖEB
HAFEN
WERFT
Internet Café
Old Prison
MANDUME NDEMUFAYO
Kabelmesse
Palm Beach
KOCH
Haus Garnison
Railway Station
TO WINDHOEK
Mole
Swimming Pool
Spar
Kristall Galerie
Swakopmund
Papa's & Diamond Jack's Jazz & Blues
THEO-BEN GURIRAB AVE
Museum
State House
DANIEL TJONGARERO AVE
DR SAM NUJOMA AVE
Schweizerhaus
Hansa
Bundu's See Hotel
Deutsches Haus
Martin Luther
ARANDIS
TREKKOPJE
WATERBANK
EBONY
AUKAS
Pension Rapmund
Omeg Haus
Snake Park
Charlotte's Guesthouse
Wildlife Conservation Library
OTAVI
ALBERTINA AMATHILA AVE
Duneside Guesthouse
Swakop Lodge Grüner Kranz
LÜDERITZ
ANTON LUBOWSKI AVE
Jetty
Hohenzollernhaus
Sculteтus House
Sam's Giardino
Europa Hof
D'Avignon
NATHANIEL MAXUILILI
RHODE ALLEE
Prinzessin-Rupprecht-Heim
Youth Hostel
Cemetery
WINDHUKER
STRAND
SWAKOP
Swakop Rest Camp
Swakop River
National Marine Aquarium
Garni Adler
M 500
Yd 500
TO WALVIS BAY

English is Namibia's official language, but German is widely used ... and Swakop residents in particular are well-versed in the language.

Swakopmund

RUNNING OUT OF STEAM
One of Swakop's most famous pieces of history lies just outside of town – nicknamed 'Martin Luther', the now rusty old steam engine was imported from Hamburg in Germany to take the place of oxen who struggled in the heat.

NATIONAL MARINE AQUARIUM
Hand-feeding by divers, an underwater walkway through the huge main tank and a wide array of local marine life (ranging from sharks to crayfish) make Swakop's aquarium a good place to spend half an hour or longer.

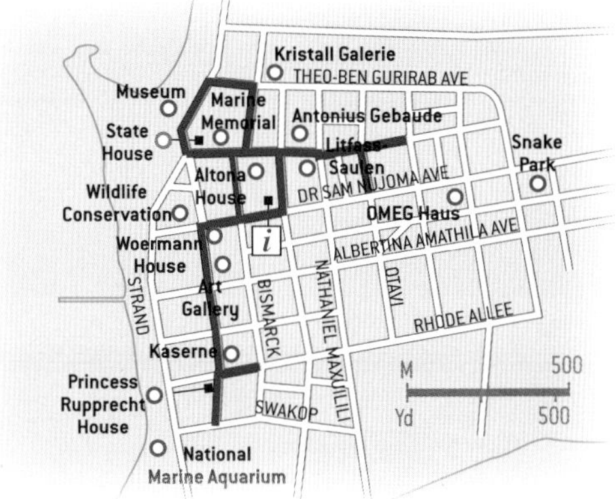

SWAKOP RIVER DELTA
A couple of hundred metres from the aquarium is the Swakop River Delta, an excellent spot for bird-watching and bird photography (including flamingo, pelican, cormorants and kestrels), with a 4km river trail for walkers.

> ***Top Tip***
> *A short drive out of town are sand dunes that are ideal for adventure sports (4x4, dune-boarding, quad biking) as well as the Welwitschia Drive in the Namib-Naukluft Park.*

The old jetty, originally built in 1911 during the German colonial era.

THE ABOMINABLE JETTY
Swakop's well-known iron jetty stretches 262m into the ocean but is now unfortunately dilapidated, has been closed to the public and exists merely as a landmark rather than a tourist 'attraction'. The lighthouse can be seen from as far as 30km away – a good thing considering how treacherous Namibia's Skeleton Coast has been over the last century.

HARBOURING NO BAD FEELINGS
Swakop was founded by the Germans in 1892 in order to match the British who had already established their own 'port presence' at Walvis Bay on the strategically valuable Skeleton Coast. Sadly, Swakop proved a poor choice, as the harbour was prone to silting up. Just 14 years later the government hoped the construction of a mole would help to create an artificial harbour that could function properly. Regrettably, sandbanks built up and ruined any chance for the harbour. On a more positive note, it did improve the safety and bathing pleasure for beach users and the mole is now used as a launching spot for boats and small craft. It also allows walkers the chance to see dolphins at close range.

Swakopmund is a good base for visiting the dramatic Spitzkoppe, which are just over 100km away from town.

Walvis Bay's huge saltwater lagoon is a vital habitat for the flamingoes that flock there in their thousands all year round.

Walvis Bay

The long, straight and rolling road between Walvis Bay and Swakopmund.

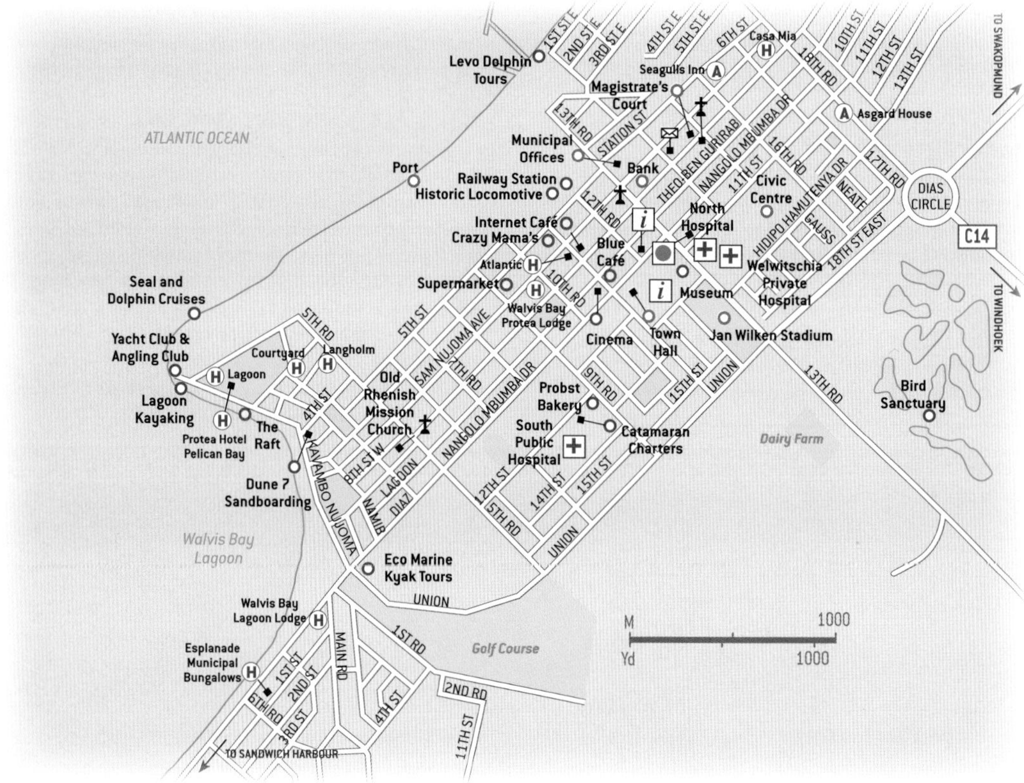

Namibia's best natural harbour (and only deepwater port), Walvis is a vital base for patrolling the valuable fishing ground and offshore diamond fields.

Walvis Bay

Walvis Bay lies 30km south of Swakopmund, and many visitors stay in Swakop and journey down to Walvis to partake in the bird-watching (numerous sea birds, including the favourite flamingoes and pelicans), angling, seal-spotting cruises offshore (if you're in luck you'll get to see dolphin and even sunfish from your craft), or the more leisurely boating activities on the lagoon. The architecture of the town lacks the character of Swakop's German charm, possibly because the port was annexed by the British in 1878 (the Germans never took control of Walvis and were forced to lay port elsewhere).

Top Tip
Avoid the tourist trap of activities centred solely on the lagoon – explore some of the magnificent desert sights and scenery that surround the town. It's an experience largely untapped by visitors.

The legendary Bartolomeu Dias is down in the history books as the first European to visit here, back in 1487, and he named the spot Bay of Whales. For the next two centuries whalers and numerous other vessels dropped anchor in Walvis Bay (as well as at Sandwich Harbour), and when the Dutch came to town in 1793 they adapted its name to Walvisbaai (Walvis Bay), and some claim their influence is still felt in the town's lack of architectural character! Walvis' small population of just over 40,000 rely on fish and fishing for their livelihood, as well as salt production (Walvis supplies more than 90% of South Africa's salt). The salt is evaporated from seawater trapped in a 3500-hectare 'salt pan'. Tours of the salt works are offered by local tour operators. Walvis Bay Lagoon is one of the two most valuable wetland areas (along with the nearby Sandwich Harbour) to be found throughout the entire west coast of Africa. The lagoon is able to support more than 150,000 birds in summer and almost 70,000 in winter, notably the Greater and Lesser Flamingoes, pelicans, migrant waders and sea birds. Wait for low tide to get your best birding opportunities as the birds scour the shallow water for tasty marine morsels.

Top Tip
For a different experience, stop by the Raft Restaurant (built on stilts in the Walvis Bay lagoon) and enjoy a bite to eat or a drink at the bar. It's 'a good place to be seen'!

Top: Greater Flamingoes in flight.
Above: Pelican preening itself.

A good catch, a quiet beach, and a friend to bear witness to your success. Fisherman's paradise!

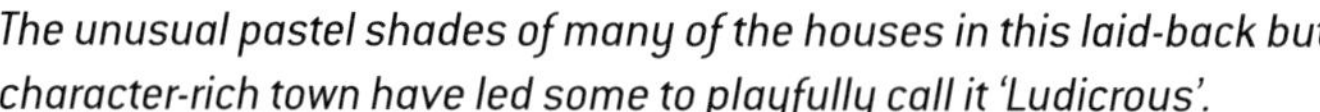

The unusual pastel shades of many of the houses in this laid-back but character-rich town have led some to playfully call it 'Ludicrous'.

Lüderitz

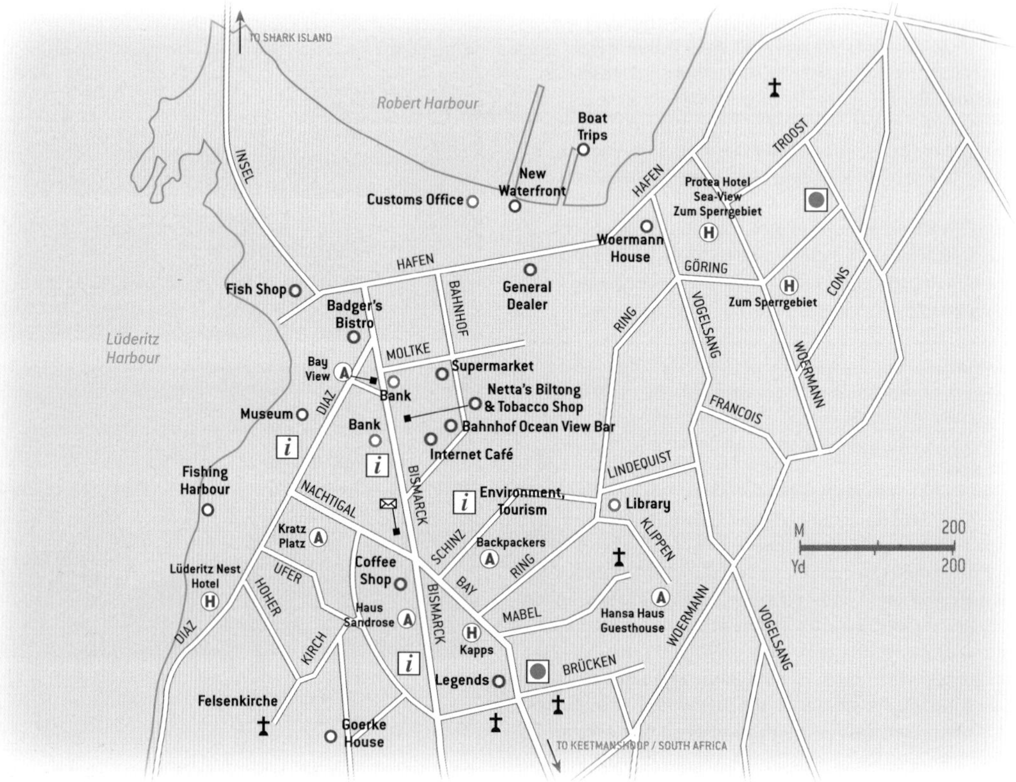

> ***Top Tip***
> *Plan your wardrobe carefully: Lüderitz's weather is 'predictably unpredictable'. Within a few hours Mother Nature might hurl sunshine, fog, cold, wind and even rain at you. Locals 'joke' that the wind is so strong it blasts the paint off cars. Joke?*

Some of Lüderitz's brightly coloured buildings.

A favourite travel destination and a stunning example of friendly, small-town and slow-paced hospitality, rich in German tradition and history, Lüderitz is worth the effort to visit for a few days. Sitting more than 360km from Keetmanshoop, Lüderitz is literally and figuratively isolated from the rest of the world. However, it's not cut off completely, as it has a rich supply of public telephones that seem to pop up on every corner. Tourism is increasing and accommodation options are happily opening up to meet the new demand, with the first phase of a new waterfront development already completed. Part of Lüderitz's charm is that its isolation for so many years has left the town with a wealth of original architecture and interesting buildings from the 1900s. Added to this is the fun nature of the town, with its eccentric house colours and the midday siren that doubles up as a fire alarm! Bartolomeu Dias also made his mark here and named the town Angra Pequena (Little Bay). A number of tools and artefacts dating back to the Stone Age confirm that the Khoi found 'Little Bay' some time before Dias! Kolmanskop and Elizabeth Bay ghost towns are a comfortable drive from Lüderitz and are both worth visiting.

Named after the six springs (ses fonteine) found here, this dusty little town in the middle of nowhere lies central to all the delights of northwest Namibia.

Sesfontein & Opuwo

SESFONTEIN ▼

Fort Sesfontein was established prior to World War I as a German army outpost to keep an eye on the area militarily as well as from a crime and gun-running perspective. Abandoned and in an awful state of deterioration for decades, it was given a face-lift and general overhaul and converted into a comfy oasis-like lodge. It's an ideal base for explorations into the surrounding Kaokoland and Damaraland. The historic graveyard is worth a wander. Take in the views of the town and its mountain backdrop from the shale and limestone hills that skirt the fort.

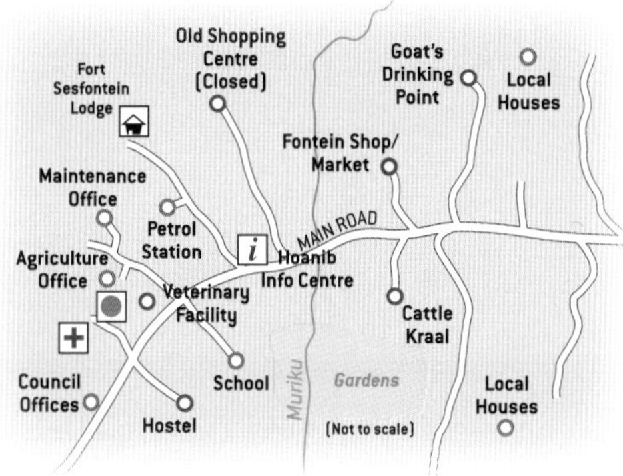

About 29km out of town is Ongongo Camp, which means 'beautiful little place', and the Blinkwater Falls back up this claim.

Otjitaimo Canyon is 10km out of town and is hard to reach on foot, yet it offers rich rewards for seekers of solitude and spectacular scenery.

> ***Top Tip***
> *A day trip along the Hoanib River from Sesfontein to Purros offers great viewing of the desert elephant as well as numerous other forms of wildlife. Please note that it is advisable to travel with a guide.*

OPUWO ▶

Opuwo means 'the end' in the native Herero tongue, which is fitting as it is a vital stocking-up point for travellers passing through – and passing through is what most people do in Opuwo, apart from using it as a base for exploring the surrounding area, which includes some nearby settlements of Himba and Herero people. Kaokoveld adventurers and explorers often use Opuwo as a stop-off point, or stop relatively near by.

Opuwo made its name as a base used by the South African troops during times of conflict and occupation

A wall of tins built by the locals in Opuwo.

in Namibia. It is an otherwise unpretentious little settlement lost in the bush and tucked away in its own small 'crater', although there are some interesting local dwellings, such as traditional rondavels (round huts) and Himba huts. Opuwo has two 'supermarkets' and a fish shop called Madiba (Nelson Mandela's nickname).

> ***Top Tip***
> *Locals will be willing to act as guides (for a fee), but they no longer think tourist cameras are worth a free smile. Be careful when encroaching on tribal land and always seek permission.*

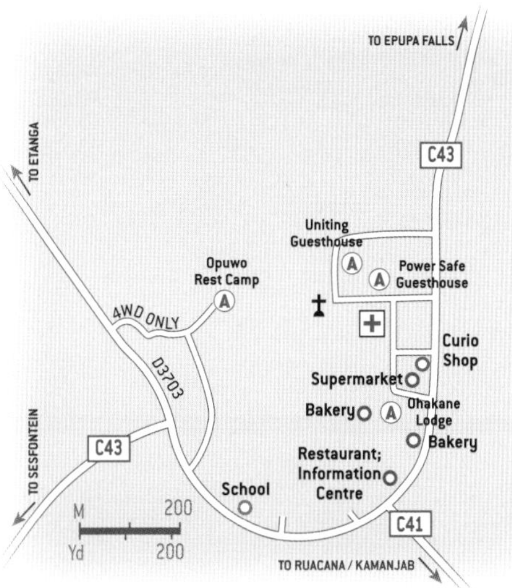

Rundu presents weary Caprivi-bound travellers with a relative oasis to wash away the bleak desert landscape through which they have travelled.

Oshakati & Rundu

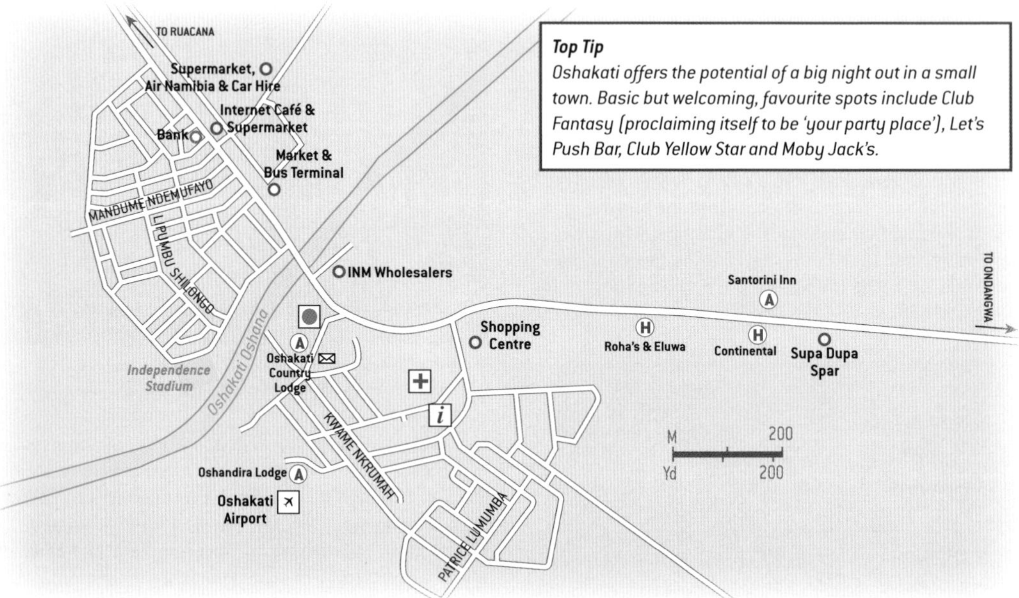

Top Tip

Oshakati offers the potential of a big night out in a small town. Basic but welcoming, favourite spots include Club Fantasy (proclaiming itself to be 'your party place'), Let's Push Bar, Club Yellow Star and Moby Jack's.

OSHAKATI ▲

Big and spread out, Oshakati is primarily a residential and governmental town, hosting the Northern Campus of the University of Namibia, some private schools and municipal buildings. There are many comfortable homes in town, but equally there are areas which offer more basic housing and services.

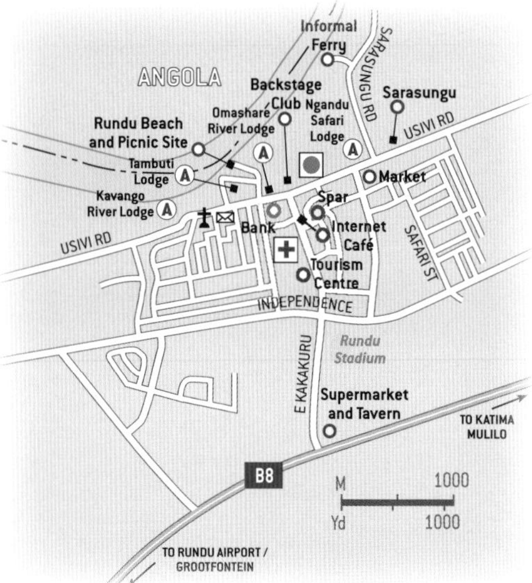

RUNDU ▼

Situated above the Kavango (Okavango in Botswana) River flood plain, Rundu is a fabulous stopover en route to more entertaining and enjoyable activities or destinations in the Kavango and Caprivi regions. Its proximity to Angola has given the little outpost of Rundu a Portuguese flavour mixed with a languid sense of calm. There are great views across the Kavango River, with some water sports, fishing and 4x4 opportunities for the energetic. Rundu is an important refuelling stop for travellers: petrol is scarce in the area, and the town's bottle stores present shoppers with a fantastic array of products. Souvenir hunters will enjoy Rundu's happy hunting grounds: woodcarving in the area has a proud tradition.

Woodcarvings for sale in Rundu.

The patron saint of mine workers (believe it or not) is St Barbara ... and you'll find Tsumeb's St Barbara Catholic Church on Main Street.

Katima Mulilo & Tsumeb

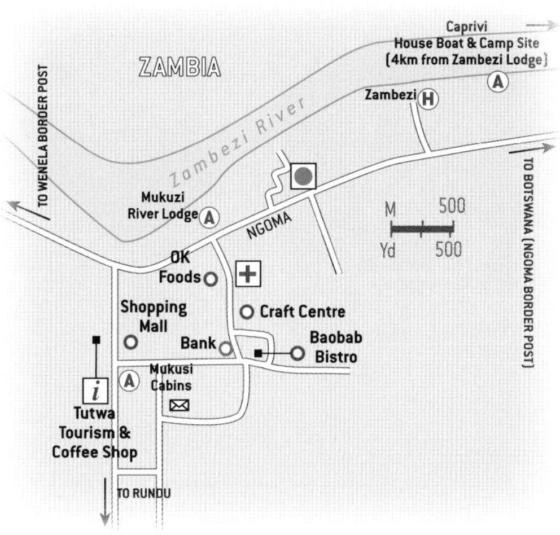

KATIMA MULILO ▲

Katima Mulilo boasts excellent facilities for travellers and is a great base for exploring as well as embarking on adventure activities. Located on the banks of the mighty Zambezi River, it provides an easy base from which to hop into Zambia, Zimbabwe or Botswana.

TSUMEB ▼

Tsumeb is attractive, with wide, quiet streets blessed with beautiful old colonial buildings and dressed with

The mokoro (dugout), a popular means of transport in the wetlands.

jacaranda, bougainvillea, palm trees, parks and lawns. Tsumeb's name can be translated to mean 'to dig a hole in loose ground', which is understandable given its status as one of Namibia's key mining towns. The crystals and gemstones unearthed here have earned the town a worldwide reputation. The Tsumeb Museum affords visitors a fantastic window into the past, while the Tsumeb Cultural Village is an open-air museum that allows visitors to glimpse first-hand what tribal life is all about in Namibia.

> ***Top Tip***
> *It's rough and ready for most big city folk; local eateries include The Butchy-Butchy Bakery (offering freshly baked bread) or you can rub shoulders with the local Crocodile Dundees at Mad Dog McGee's (a meat-eater's haven).*

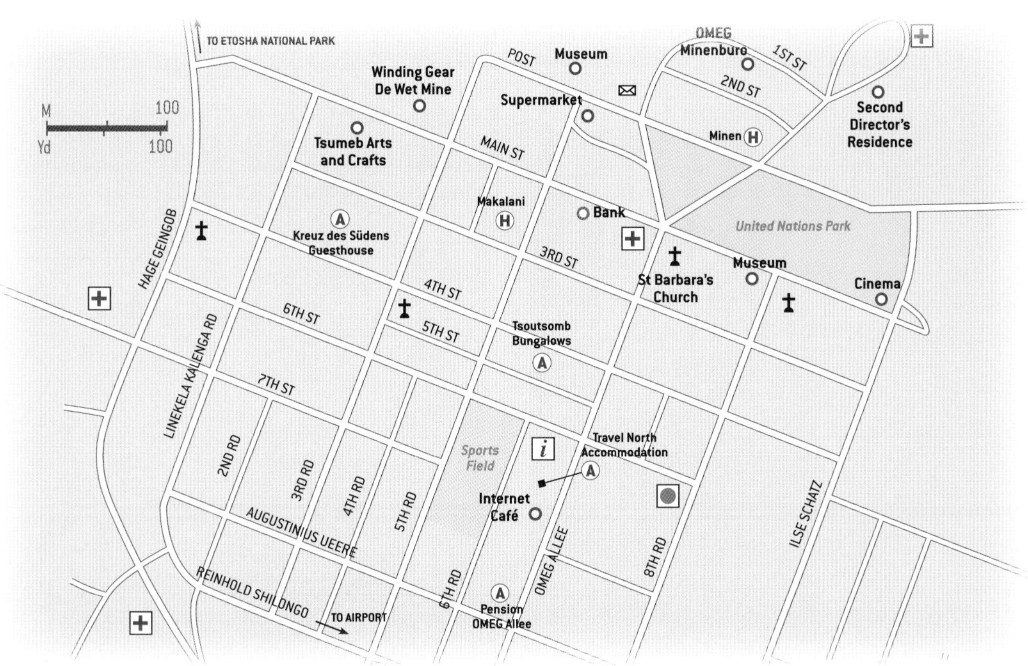

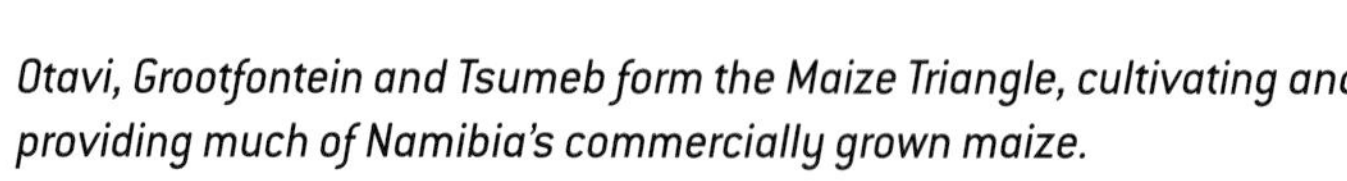

Otavi, Grootfontein and Tsumeb form the Maize Triangle, cultivating and providing much of Namibia's commercially grown maize.

Grootfontein & Otavi

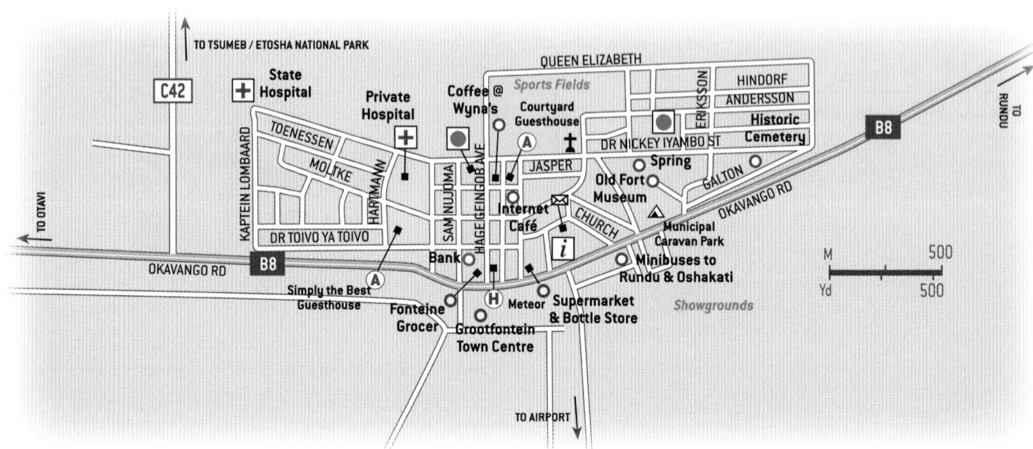

GROOTFONTEIN ▲

Meaning 'large fountain' (there are strong natural springs in Tree Park), Grootfontein offers a pleasant stopover, as trees line the streets and limestone buildings stand proudly amid the spring explosions of jacaranda and red flamboyants.

The fascinating Old Fort Museum (signposted as Die Alte Feste) off Eriksson Street has interesting historic photographs, gems, rocks and a display on the old art of wagon and cart manufacture. Straussen Ostrich Farm offers an insight into the ostrich industry, and includes a shop and a restaurant. The Hoba meteorite – the largest recorded meteorite on earth at around 60 tonnes – can be found 50km outside town. Almost three metres square (and 75–122cm thick!), it may have celebrated in the region of 200 to 400 million birthdays, and it found its home here around 80,000 years ago.

The enormous Hoba meteorite that landed near Grootfontein many thousands of years ago.

OTAVI ▼

Otavi's natural springs play a vital role in irrigating the surrounding farmlands, and it's no surprise that the name translates to 'place of water'. The town made its name during the copper-mining boom years at the turn of the last century, and an amethyst mine is found just out of town.

Otavi hit the headlines with the 1991 discovery of the jawbone of a prehistoric ape-like creature dubbed the 'Otavi Ape', a creature which no doubt spent some time in the abundant caves in the area – anyone with an interest in caves will enjoy a great deal of time 'caving' themselves.

> ***Top Tip***
> *A 2km drive out of Otavi will bring you to the Khorab Memorial. Erected in 1920, it marks the spot where the German forces capitulated to General Louis Botha's South African forces in 1915.*

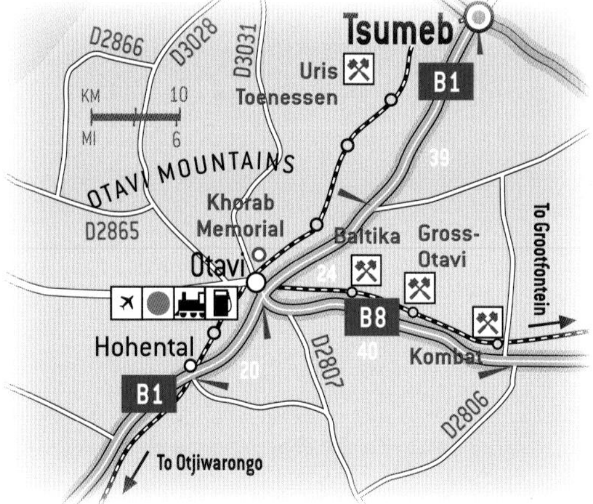

Outjo means (appropriately) 'a place on the rocks', while Otjiwarongo was named by the Herero who thought of it as the 'place of the fat cattle'.

Otjiwarongo & Outjo

> ***Top Tip***
> *An hour or so outside of Otjiwarongo are a number of fossilised footprints that date back 200 million years! Stare in awe at the massive set of prints made by a very large two-legged dinosaur.*

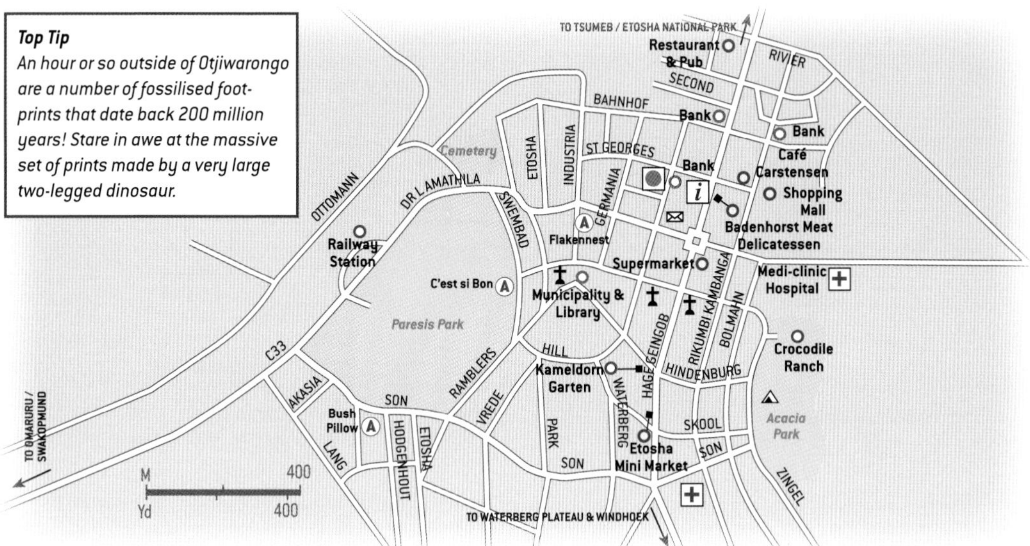

OTJIWARONGO ▲
Known for its spring explosions of jacaranda and bougainvillea, Otjiwarongo is situated close to the Waterberg Plateau Park. Otjiwarongo boasts Namibia's first crocodile ranch, which serves meals to visitors, sells meat to locals and exports skins to Asia. Look out for the famous Locomotive No. 41 at the train station ... but don't rush to catch it! Since 1960 it hasn't gone anywhere as the railway gauge was changed from narrow to 1.067mm gauge.

OUTJO ▼
Outjo revolves around cattle-ranching and one-night-stay tourists en route to Etosha National Park, Khorixas or northern Kaokoland.

One of the town's most outstanding (literally) landmarks is the Water Tower, which has stood tall since 1901. The town museum is in Franke House, which dates back to 1899 and was one of Outjo's first homes. The museum shows off a wide range of minerals and gemstones, local history artefacts, and numerous animal skins, bones and horns – and has a one-of-a-kind sheep-sheering device that operates off a bicycle chain! The hills of nearby Ugab Terrace offer spectacular rock formations, including shapes like medieval castles. Gamkarab Cave (50km away) boasts stalagmites and stalagtites of distinction.

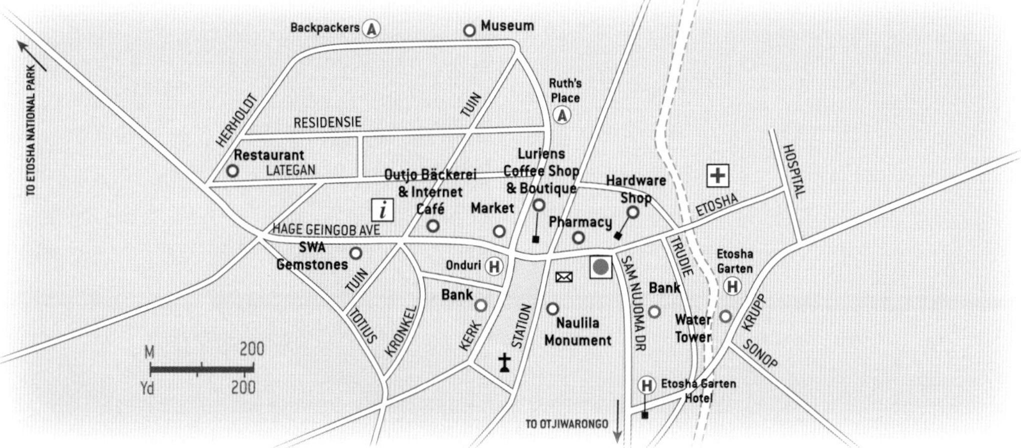

Omaruru's name is derived from a somewhat unfortunate Herero description of cattle milk, omaere omruru, *or bitter curd.*

Omaruru & Henties Bay

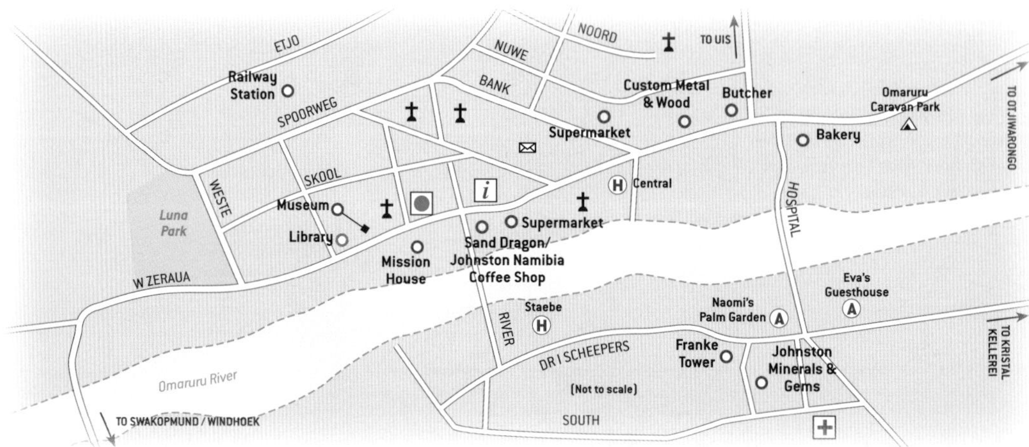

OMARURU ▲

A dry river (most of the year) runs through the surprisingly green and pretty town of Omaruru. The major attraction in town is Franke Tower, which proudly commemorates the German captain who helped to repel the Hereros in 1904. More of the town's early history can be viewed in the museum at Mission House, Omaruru's oldest building.

On the outskirts of town is the Kristall Kellerei (*kellerei* means 'cellars'), Namibia's first winery. Omaruru and its surroundings offer good birding opportunities, especially the possibility of ticking off some of the northwestern endemics. Several game lodges in the area (which offer luxury accommodation) have been stocked with a wide variety of antelope, giraffe and rhino. The Erongo Massif near Omaruru is an excellent spot for rock climbers.

HENTIES BAY ▼

Hentie van der Merwe first started fishing here in 1929, and little did he know that a town would grow here and adopt his name. A sleepy hollow, Henties wakes up for the summer season to welcome the 10,000-plus visitors who flock to this fisherman's paradise, many with an eye on casting a line into the ocean or swinging their clubs at the nine-hole golf course that runs through a valley down towards the beach. The town has plenty of petrol stations to cater for the lack of supply further north.

Cape fur seals line the rocks and sand at Cape Cross, 60km north of Henties Bay.

Okahandja is renowned for offering some of the best fresh vegetables in Namibia, while Gobabis produces a third of the country's red meat.

Gobabis & Okahandja

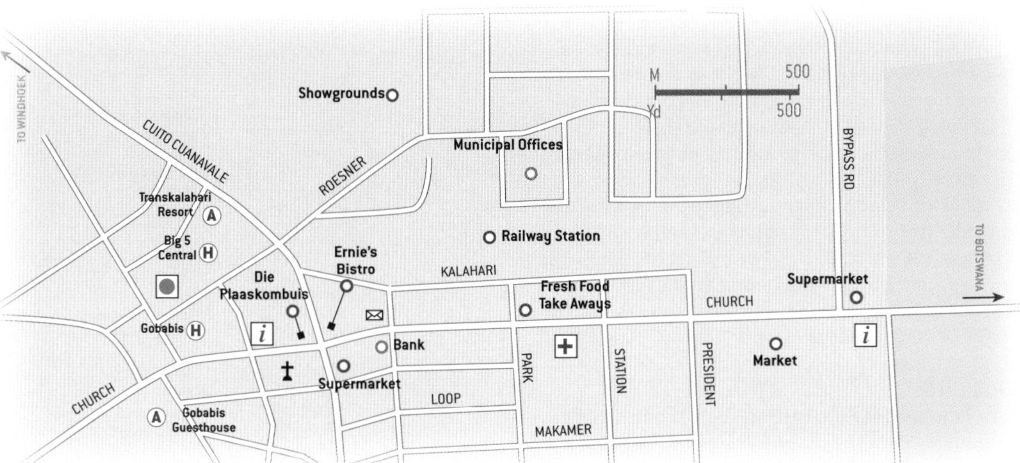

GOBABIS ▲
Gobabis has a special charm for passing tourists on this vital route through to Botswana. There are pretty old church buildings in town and a golf course. A statue of a bull at the town's western entrance bears testament to the importance of cattle to the Omaheke region, which has the second-highest number of cattle in all of Namibia's 13 regions.

> ***Top Tip***
> *The old experimental tobacco station in Okahandja is a photogenic building. It was started up in 1906 and people hoped to capitalise on planting tobacco and rolling out cigars. Operations have long since ceased and the building is now empty and overgrown.*

Herero woman.

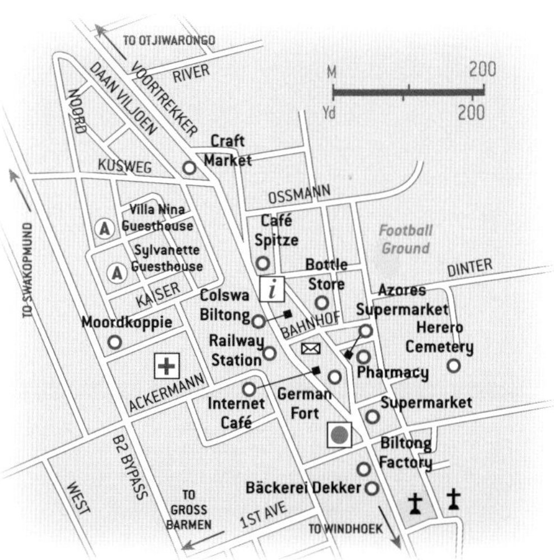

◀ OKAHANDJA
Okahandja might be small, but it boasts some of Namibia's finest open-air markets specialising in souvenirs such as woodcarvings (notably enormous hippos, huge giraffe and up to 2m tall human busts) as well as art from all around Namibia, Zimbabwe and even central Africa. The administrative 'capital' of the Herero, Okahandja hosts a large and colourful annual festival in August to honour the Herero forefathers. Okahandja is set in excellent farming country. There are numerous historic sights in and around town, including Moordkoppie (Murder Hill, the scene of the 1850 Herero massacre) and many graves of influential local leaders from the last 100 years (including that of the Oorlam leader Jan Jonker Afrikaner).

Rehoboth's hot springs were called anhes *(smoke) by the Swartbooi Namas because of the steam that rises from the hot water.*

Mariental & Rehoboth

MARIENTAL ▼

Forget about peace and tranquility here: Mariental suffers from an unhappy climate. The heat is atrocious in summer, the cold is biting in winter, and the changes in season bring strong winds that blow dust everywhere. Local industry focuses on cultivating animal fodder, fruit and vegetables, as well as ostrich meat and karakul pelts, aided by its proximity to the Hardap Dam (Namibia's largest reservoir). Hardap itself is enjoyed by anglers, hikers, birders and boating enthusiasts. The town owes its name to Herman Brandt, the first colonial settler in the area, who made his wife happy by naming it Marie's Valley (hence Mariental).

REHOBOTH ▶

You have to see the Rehoboth Museum (built in 1903, and found behind the post office) – partly because there are few other attractions in town. Aside from a fascinating collection and display of bank notes and various items of local history, flora and fauna, you'll find a good history of the proud Baster people for whom Rehoboth is now their cultural home.

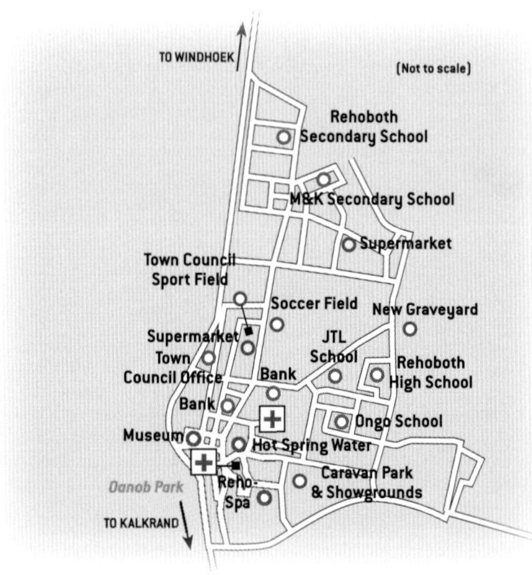

> ***Top Tip***
> *Rehoboth's spa offers a pleasant hot spring enjoyed by the Nama for centuries, though now somewhat the worse for wear. Lake Oanob Resort is becoming increasingly popular for water sports, hiking and bird-watching.*

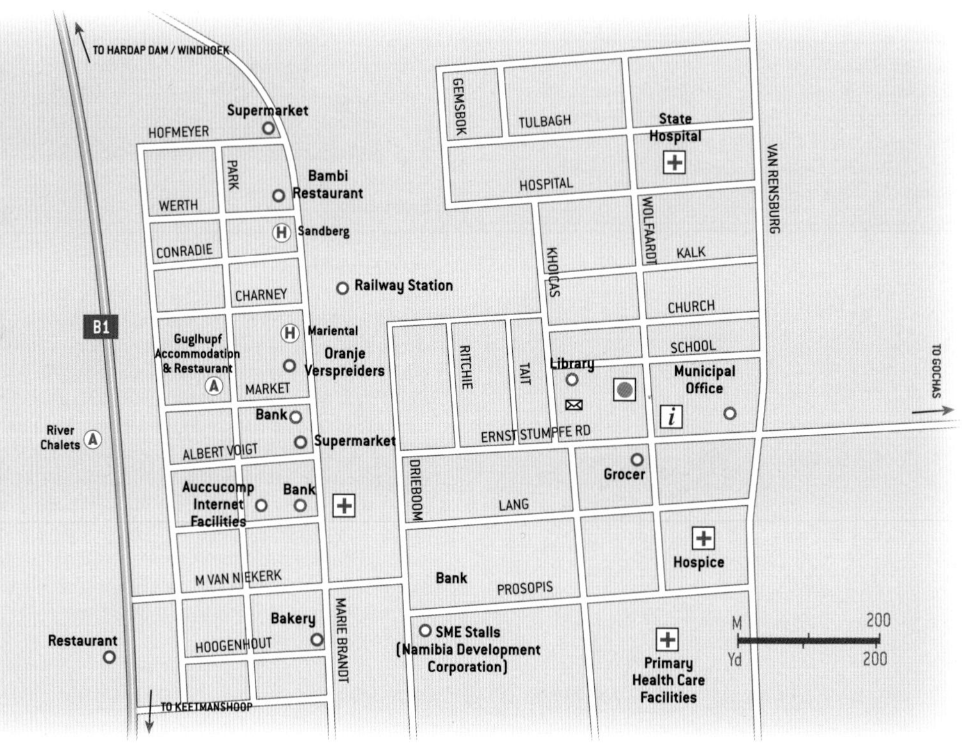

The hub of the karakul wool industry, Keetmanshoop is the 'capital of the south' and its road junction links Lüderitz, South Africa and Windhoek.

Keetmanshoop

KEETMANSHOOP

Keetmanshoop (shortened to 'Keet' by the locals) is a sunny town with attractive German colonial architecture, pretty gardens and a rustic museum. 'Keet' is situated almost 500km south of Windhoek and roughly 1000m above sea level. The original church was built in 1866 but, alas, 24 years later a freak flood washed the entire building away. Its replacement (the current town museum) was put up five years later – this time on somewhat higher ground!

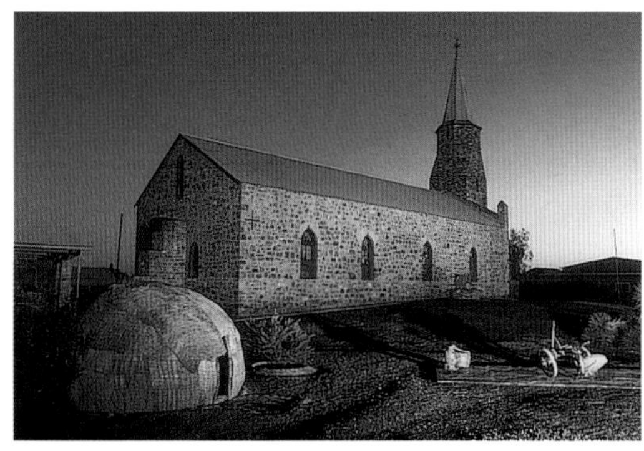

Keetmanshoop Museum.

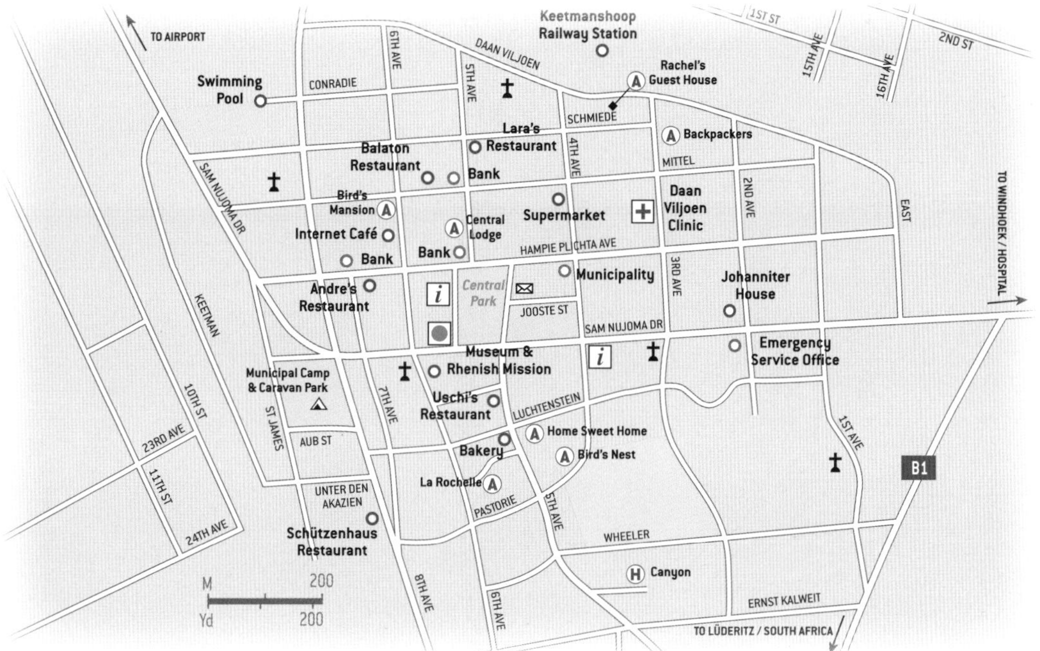

Key Tourist Areas

Key Tourist Areas

Namibia represents an uneasy compromise between man and nature to carve out their territory of choice. Jagged and – in places – treacherous natural borders were created by centuries of persistent erosion by the mighty Atlantic Ocean, while the top and bottom of this vast land have been chipped away by great rivers with memories deeper than humankind: the Orange, Kunene, Kavango, Zambezi and Chobe. Where nature failed to penetrate the remaining borders, man stepped in to rule straight lines of territorial control. This strange shape for such a stark yet hauntingly beautiful land befits a country that has seen much pain and suffering. It's as though someone had tried to tame the land, but nature reminds travellers and settlers that it can't be harnessed, can't be approached lightly or without caution. It allows man to take dangerous liberties as his pride and courage urge him to conquer the elements. Yet always Namibia will win. This is a land which is a great ally, but an even greater enemy.

Etosha ('great white place' in Herero, due to the bright sun) is one of the finest game reserves to be found in Southern Africa.

Etosha National Park

Etosha is a vital game reserve for the entire Southern Africa region and is home to 114 species of mammal, 340 bird species, 110 different reptiles, 16 species of amphibians and yet just one fish species. All this is found in the 22,000km^2 that makes up the park named after the massive pan that covers a vast 5000km^2, stretching roughly 120km from east to west and some 70km across at its widest point. The pan seldom boasts much water (if any) as it is fed by the rains rather than reliable rivers, and even when the rains fall hard few areas fill up or flood due to the incredibly high rate of evaporation. The rainy season signals the arrival of summer migrants in the form of mammals and birds.

Oryx (or gemsbok) tend to congregate around Etosha's water holes.

Etosha is best explored in your own car without a guide. The roads are good and the open landscape allows for excellent wildlife spotting.

Etosha National Park

In good years the pan will be alive with thousands of flamingoes. The western reaches of Etosha feature some unique areas, including the fascinating Moringa Forest or Haunted Forest (dubbed *Sprokieswoud* in Afrikaans) with its weirdly contorted moringa trees – possibly shaped by browsing herds of elephant and giraffe. Etosha has three main rest camps (Namutoni, Halali and Okaukuejo) with perimeter fencing and superb floodlit water holes which are open 24 hours a day. The world's largest game reserve until the 1960s, when its surface area was reduced by nearly 80%, Etosha remains one of the largest and most important parks in Africa.

A lioness defending her territory. She also has to do the bulk of the hunting to feed the pride.

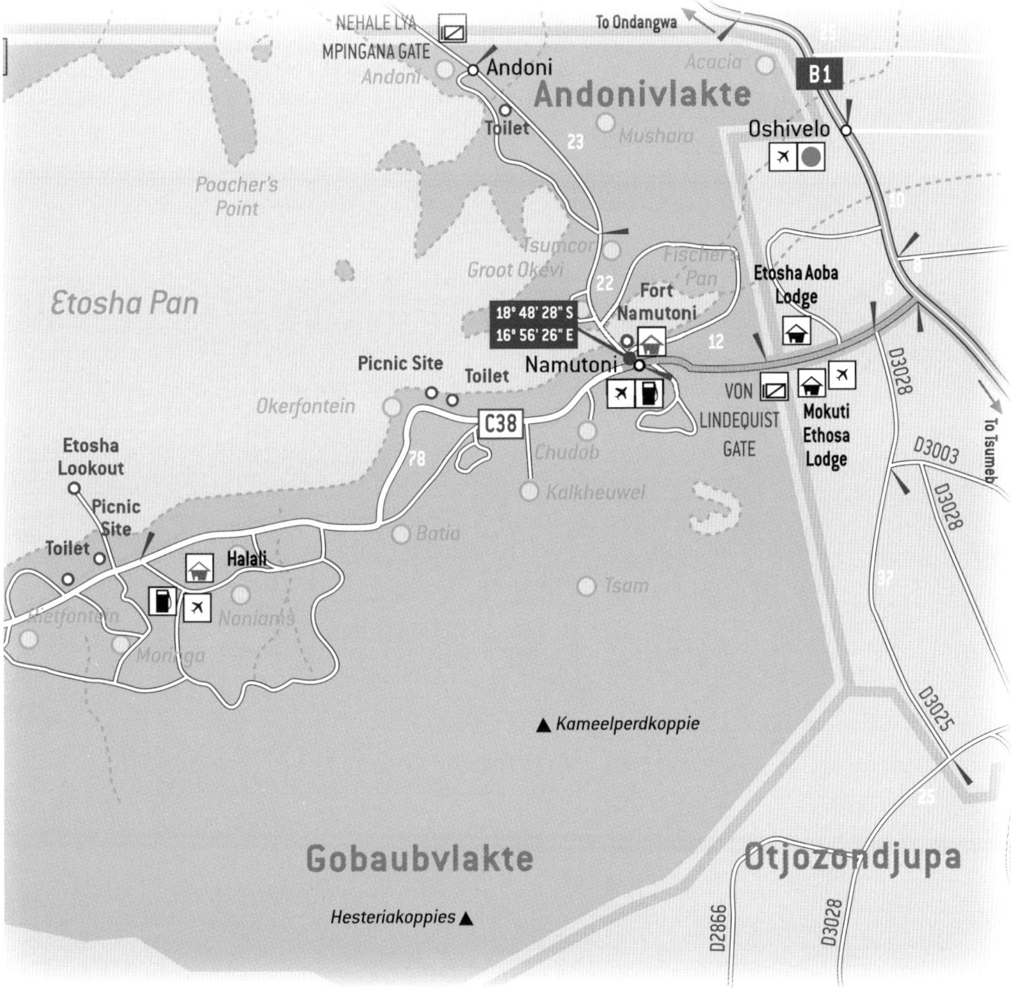

NEHALE LYA MPINGANA GATE
To Ondangwa
Andoni
Andonivlakte
Acacia
B1
Toilet
Mushara
Oshivelo
Poacher's Point
Tsumcor
Groot Okevi
Fischer's Pan
Etosha Aoba Lodge
Etosha Pan
Fort Namutoni
18° 48' 28" S
16° 56' 26" E
Namutoni
Picnic Site
Toilet
Okerfontein
C38
VON LINDEQUIST GATE
Mokuti Ethosa Lodge
D3028
To Tsumeb
D3003
Chudob
Kalkheuwel
Etosha Lookout
Picnic Site
Toilet
Halali
Batia
Tsam
Rietfontein
Noniams
Moringa
D3025
Kameelperdkoppie
Gobaubvlakte
Otjozondjupa
Hesteriakoppies
D2866
D3028

The name Naukluft means 'narrow ravine'. This dramatic landscape is much loved by hikers, 4x4 enthusiasts and photographers alike.

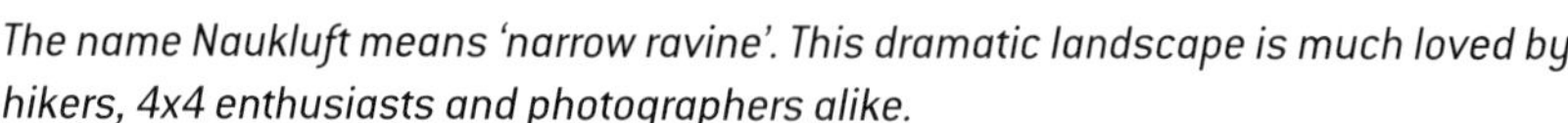

Sossusvlei, Namib-Naukluft

Sossusvlei's Dead Pan is surrounded by dunes and filled with long-dead trees.

Larger than Switzerland, the 50,000km^2-plus of fantastically scenic desert landscape occupied by the Namib-Naukluft Park ranks it with the biggest in all of Africa. It represents a vital conservation effort to retain the pristine nature of the Namib Desert, which vies with the Atacama Desert in South America for the title of oldest on earth. You'll need plenty of time to enjoy all that the park has to offer, so keep your itinerary flexible. The Namib has an amazing array of wildlife, with many plants found in the mountainous region, an area enjoyed by the rare Hartmann's mountain zebra as well as leopards and other shy animals who appreciate the vegetation and sanctuary offered by the many caves, gorges and the rocky terrain. There are also numerous small nocturnal delights (insects and reptiles) to be found throughout the area, while bird-watchers will delight in the bustling air traffic around the deep kloof which has water throughout the year. Horse riding and hiking are popular ways to traverse much of this region, with hikes ranging from a few hours up to the more advanced eight-day, 120km Naukluft Hiking Trail.

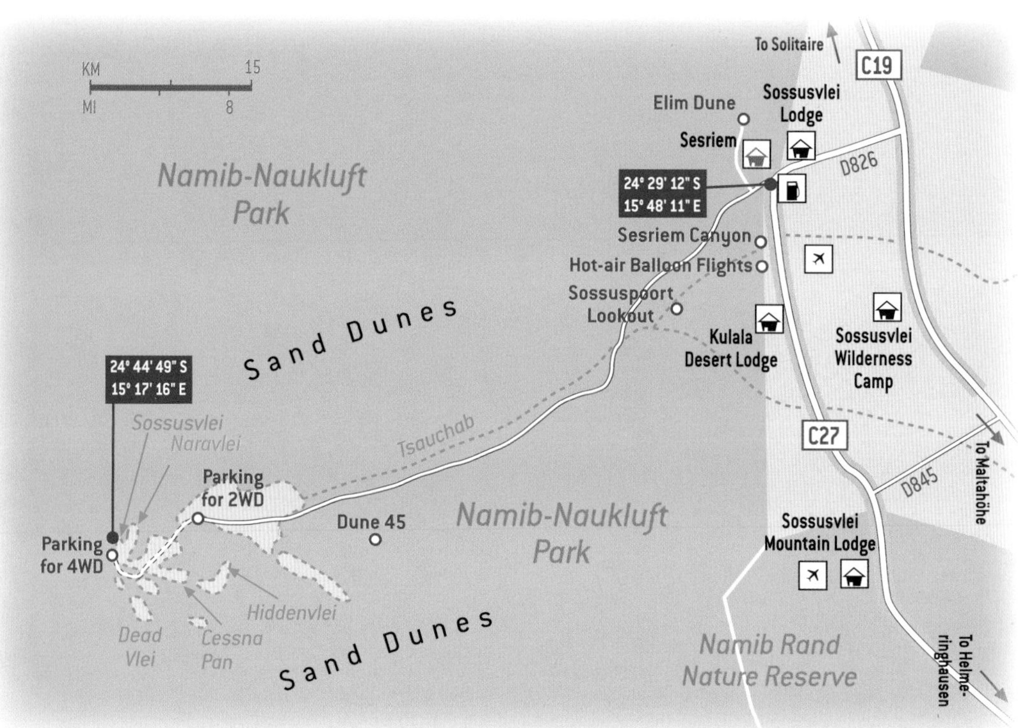

Sesriem Canyon derives its name from ses riem (six thongs), the number of rope lengths needed to draw water from the 30m deep gorge.

Sossusvlei, Namib-Naukluft

Sossusvlei, with its stark yet striking beauty, is one of the natural world's great photo opportunities. The occasional rain quickly sinks into the thirsty ground – it sustains hardy camel-thorn acacias and the indestructible *!nara*, a melon-bearing plant that offers vital nourishment to a variety of animals in this unforgiving territory. The skeletal remains of ancient trees in Dead Vlei (some of which lived centuries ago) are all that remains of easier times, when rain was more plentiful and sustained a variety of flora. Lovers of sand and dunes will be in their element at Sossusvlei as the vlei (pan) is surrounded by some of the world's tallest sand dunes. These can rise 300m and are best viewed as the early morning sun breaks the horizon, highlighting the redness of the sand. The sand at Sesriem (which acts as the gateway to Sossusvlei) is ocean sand blown inland. A number of camps, lodges and camp sites allow visitors quick access (by foot, 4x4 or shuttle) to this dramatic landscape with its great walking opportunities and fascinating geological formations.

Sossusvlei, alive with colour.

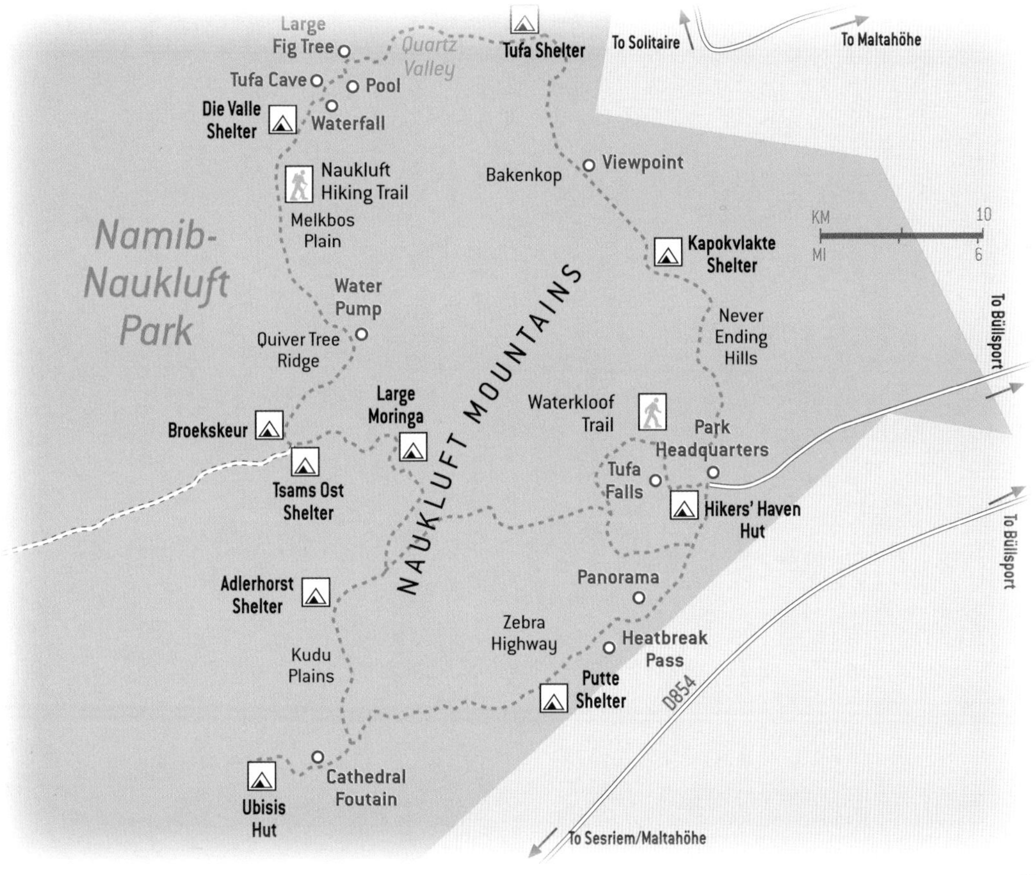

Large Fig Tree
Quartz Valley
Tufa Shelter
To Solitaire
To Maltahöhe
Tufa Cave
Pool
Die Valle Shelter
Waterfall
Naukluft Hiking Trail
Bakenkop
Viewpoint
Namib-Naukluft Park
Melkbos Plain
Kapokvlakte Shelter
KM 10
MI 6
Water Pump
Quiver Tree Ridge
Never Ending Hills
To Büllsport
NAUKLUFT MOUNTAINS
Large Moringa
Waterkloof Trail
Broekskeur
Park Headquarters
Tsams Ost Shelter
Tufa Falls
Hikers' Haven Hut
To Büllsport
Adlerhorst Shelter
Panorama
Zebra Highway
Heatbreak Pass
Kudu Plains
Putte Shelter
D854
Ubisis Hut
Cathedral Foutain
To Sesriem/Maltahöhe

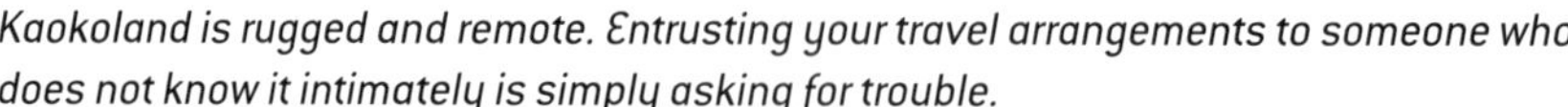

Kaokoland is rugged and remote. Entrusting your travel arrangements to someone who does not know it intimately is simply asking for trouble.

Kaokoland

The Kaokoland presents one of Namibia's greatest challenges: a vast stretch of land that is alluring yet utterly inhospitable to all but the local Himbas and extremely well-prepared travellers. Located in northwest Namibia, Kaokoland is an extremely barren mountain desert region, offering little in the way of water or vegetation, yet despite its desolation it displays a unique beauty. Its floral delights are spectacular, bottle trees rising from rocky koppies (hills) boldly defying the elements. Look closely and tread carefully and you will discover a wide range of succulents underfoot. Animals are scarce, the legacy of unscrupulous hunting, poaching and the unfortunate large-scale slaughter of wildlife for food during the desperate struggle for independence. If you're in luck you'll come across cheetah, leopard and lion, or some of the small herds of springbok and gemsbok, in addition to zebra and giraffe. The area is perhaps more famed for the presence of black rhino (Kaokoland is the black rhino's last free-roaming area on earth) and the desert elephant. These hardy elephants have extra-long legs to help them trudge the barren land, up to 70km a day, looking for nourishment. They can survive for up to five days without water.

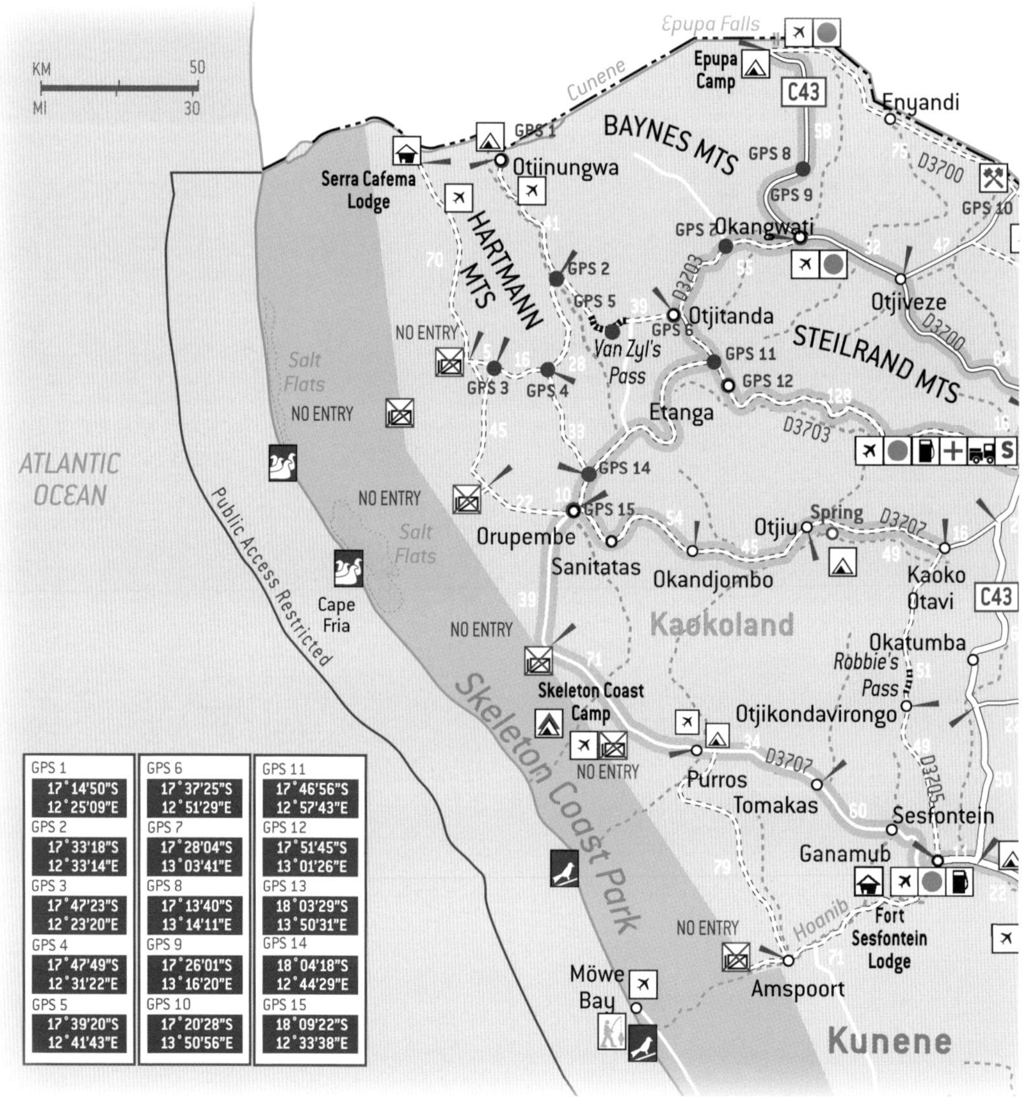

GPS	Latitude	Longitude
GPS 1	17°14'50"S	12°25'09"E
GPS 2	17°33'18"S	12°33'14"E
GPS 3	17°47'23"S	12°23'20"E
GPS 4	17°47'49"S	12°31'22"E
GPS 5	17°39'20"S	12°41'43"E
GPS 6	17°37'25"S	12°51'29"E
GPS 7	17°28'04"S	13°03'41"E
GPS 8	17°13'40"S	13°14'11"E
GPS 9	17°26'01"S	13°16'20"E
GPS 10	17°20'28"S	13°50'56"E
GPS 11	17°46'56"S	12°57'43"E
GPS 12	17°51'45"S	13°01'26"E
GPS 13	18°03'29"S	13°50'31"E
GPS 14	18°04'18"S	12°44'29"E
GPS 15	18°09'22"S	12°33'38"E

The Kaokoland's terrain might be tough and unforgiving, but it remains fragile: some tyre tracks made decades earlier remain to this day.

Kaokoland

The area is dangerous for travellers, as the searing heat and barren environment offer little sustenance for those trapped without transport, roads often get washed away in the rain, while dry riverbeds have quicksand spots that have been known to swallow vehicles. Travellers should not consider tackling this harsh territory without at least one other vehicle in tow, an experienced navigator and meticulous planning and preparation. Aside from personal safety, be extremely sensitive to the environment when driving overland. There are numerous rough paths, but make sure that you always stick to existing tracks as this will limit the damage to vegetation and animals. Try to avoid unnecessary driving or joy-riding over sandy areas in particular. Flanked by baobabs on either side, the Kunene River to the north offers a wide range of water-based diversions to cater for all tastes and levels of courage and skill.

> ***Top Tip***
> *The Kunene River boasts numerous water-sport opportunities to cater for mild to wild interests. The surrounding vegetation (lush by Kaokoland standards!) acts like a magnet for wildlife and tourists alike.*

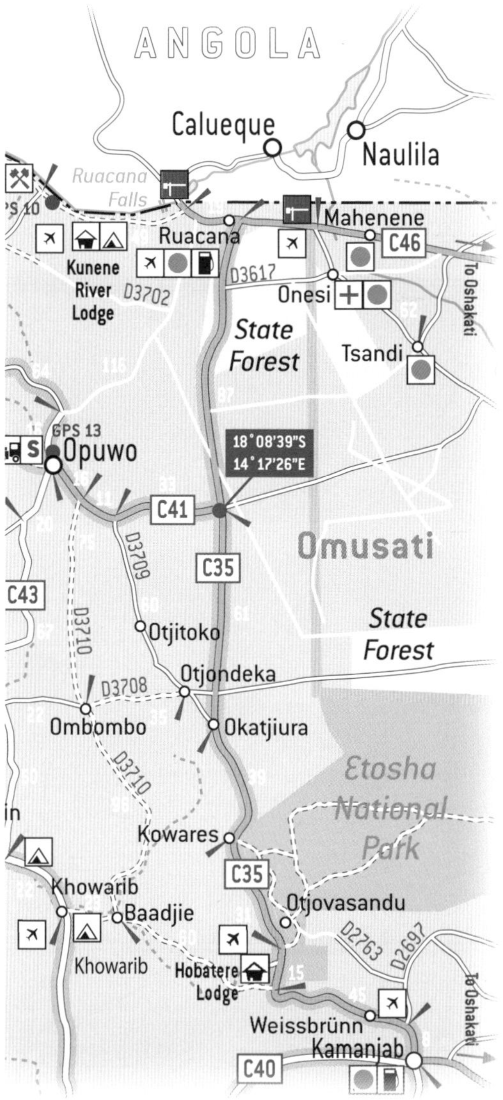

Kaokoland's varying landscapes.

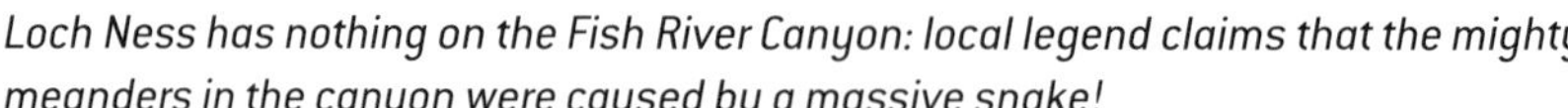

Loch Ness has nothing on the Fish River Canyon: local legend claims that the mighty meanders in the canyon were caused by a massive snake!

Fish River Canyon

One of Africa's great natural wonders (and one of the world's largest canyons, behind America's Grand Canyon), the Fish River Canyon provides an awesome spectacle as well as an abundance of adventure activities. The canyon itself is massive, 500m deep and over 25km wide in some places, and stretching a distance of around 160km. Part of the IAi-IAis conservation area, the canyon lies near Namibia's southern border, offering easy access from South Africa. The IAi-IAis rest camp, on the banks of the Fish River, accommodates most of the canyon's visitors. It is located near the hot springs in the canyon (IAi-IAis means very hot in the Nama tongue) and is surrounded by dramatic lunar-like landscape.

It is possible to visit the canyon without spending a night in IAi-IAis (if your budget or schedule is tight), as day-trips can be made from Keetmanshoop and other nearby bases. This will, however, limit the time available to explore the canyon and indulge in all the acitivities offered by lodges and rest camps in the area: horse riding, day hikes (with or without a guide), overnight hikes and camping (such as at Hobas, which is close to the canyon's main viewpoint), driving trips, animal- and bird-watching, or simple walks to the viewing spots to enjoy the unforgettable vistas. The ultimate experience is a flight over the canyon with views that go on forever – a memory that will last a lifetime. The canyon contains deposits of sandstone, shale and lava millions of years old. The geology around the canyon, and along its seemingly endless course, is fascinating, with scores of amazing rock formations, intrusive granites and dolerite dykes.

Forming the natural border between South Africa and Namibia, the Orange (or Gariep) River offers a variety of water adventures, from gently drifting down the river from one riverside camp to the next, to adrenaline-pumping white-water bashes over rocks and rapids that can challenge (and terrify) even the most experienced rivermen. River trips generally range from four to six days and can be combined with a five-day horseback trail if you have any energy and nerve left.

Right: The tiny klipspringer (half a metre at the shoulder) can elude any predator – so long as the chase is over rocky terrain. Below: A view from the bottom of the canyon.

The popular IAi-IAis hot springs oasis on the banks of the Fish River has experienced temperatures of 47 °C.

Fish River Canyon

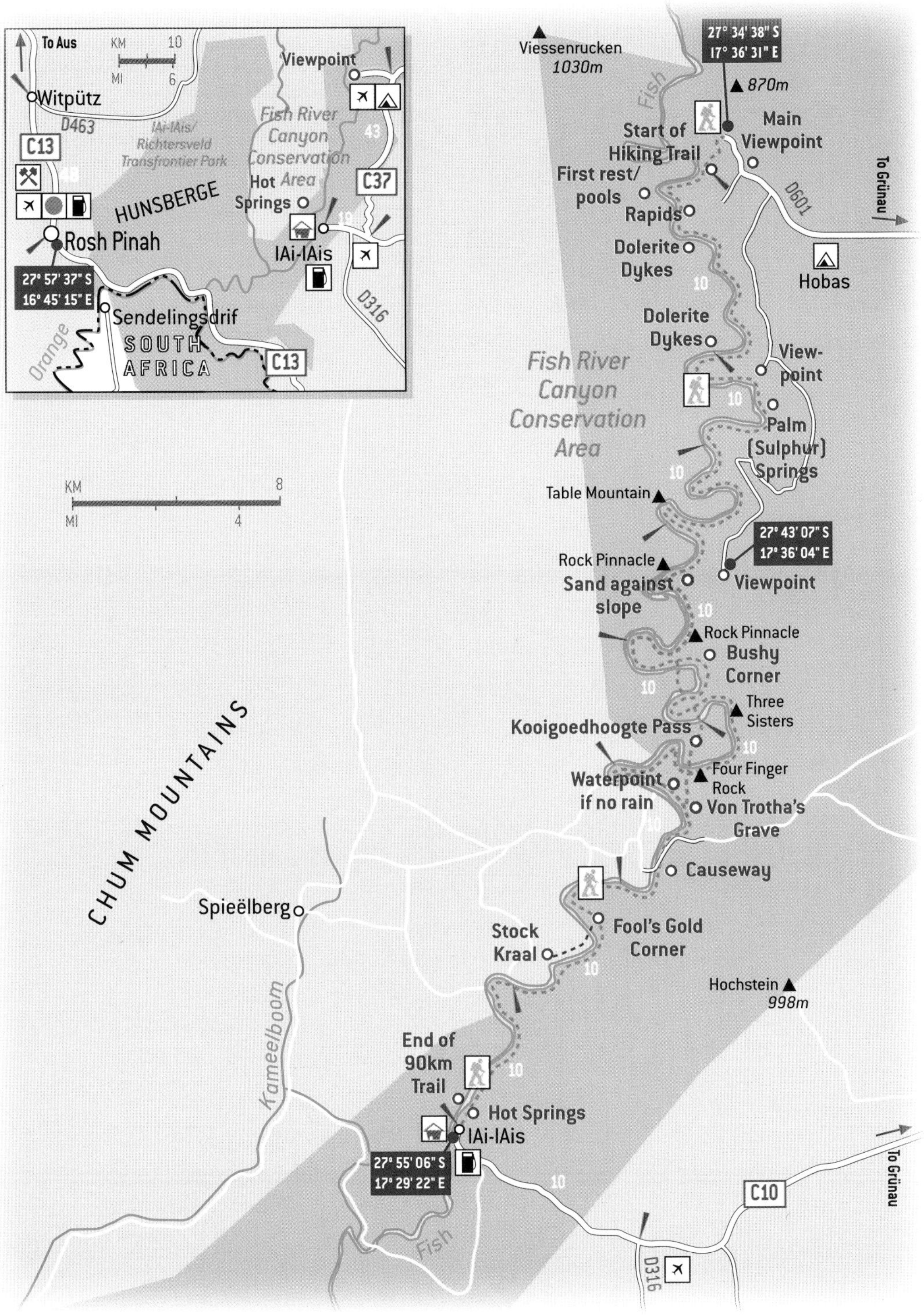

To Aus
KM 10
MI 6
Witpütz
D463
C13
IAi-IAis/ Richtersveld Transfrontier Park
HUNSBERGE
Rosh Pinah
27° 57' 37" S 16° 45' 15" E
Sendelingsdrif
Orange
SOUTH AFRICA
C13
Viewpoint
Fish River Canyon Conservation Area
43
C37
Hot Springs
19
IAi-IAis
D316

Viessenrucken 1030m
27° 34' 38" S 17° 36' 31" E
870m
Fish
Start of Hiking Trail
Main Viewpoint
First rest/ pools
Rapids
D601
To Grünau
Dolerite Dykes
Hobas
10
Dolerite Dykes
View-point
Fish River Canyon Conservation Area
Palm (Sulphur) Springs
KM 8
MI 4
Table Mountain
10
27° 43' 07" S 17° 36' 04" E
Rock Pinnacle
Sand against slope
Viewpoint
Rock Pinnacle
Bushy Corner
10
Three Sisters
Kooigoedhoogte Pass
Four Finger Rock
Waterpoint if no rain
Von Trotha's Grave
CHUM MOUNTAINS
Causeway
Spieëlberg
Stock Kraal
Fool's Gold Corner
Hochstein 998m
Kameelboom
End of 90km Trail
Hot Springs
IAi-IAis
27° 55' 06" S 17° 29' 22" E
C10
To Grünau
Fish
D316

!Nara melons, endemic to the Namib Desert, are a valuable food source for desert scavengers as well as a traditional food of the Topnaar Namas.

Namib-Naukluft Park & West Coast

The dramatic Bogenfels Arch, a 50m high rock arch south of Lüderitz on the West Coast.

Previously known as the Namib Desert Park, the Namib section of the Namib-Naukluft Park (Africa's third-largest nature reserve) offers plenty of worthwhile attractions, including the majestic cliffs and ravines of the Kuiseb Canyon, with plenty of overnight and 4x4 opportunities. Widely regarded as the oldest desert on earth, it is believed that the Namib Desert has 'enjoyed' its arid to semi-arid conditions for as long as 80 million years. The West Coast offers fantastic hiking and driving trips (especially along the Skeleton Coast), as well as excellent fishing. A treacherous coastline over the centuries, many ships have run aground here. It's harshness is typified in the landmark Bogenfels Arch which is, unfortunately, no longer accessible to the public.

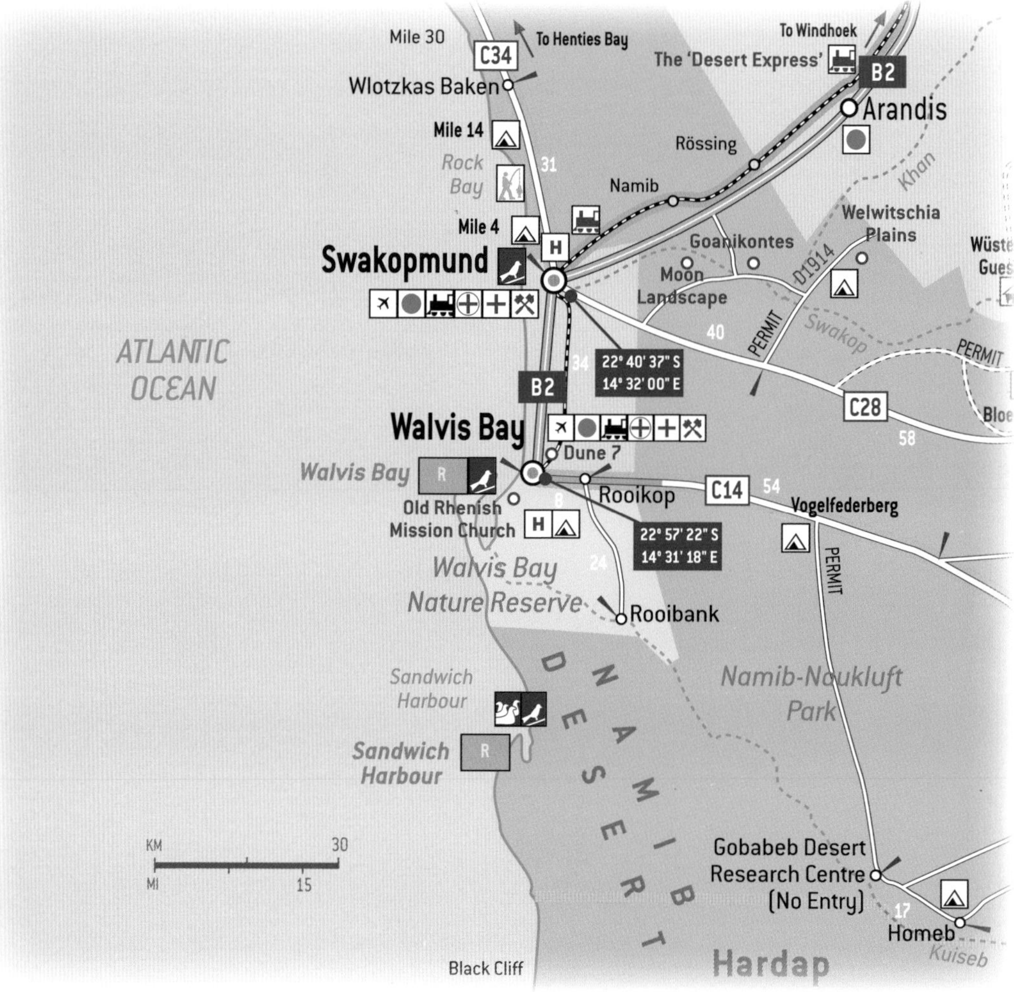

Mile 30
C34
To Henties Bay
To Windhoek
The 'Desert Express'
B2
Wlotzkas Baken
Arandis
Mile 14
Rössing
Rock Bay
31
Khan
Namib
Welwitschia Plains
Mile 4
H
Goanikontes
Swakopmund
Moon Landscape
D1914
PERMIT
Swakop
40
PERMIT
ATLANTIC OCEAN
34
22° 40' 37" S
14° 32' 00" E
B2
C28
Walvis Bay
58
Dune 7
Walvis Bay
R
Rooikop
C14
54
Old Rhenish Mission Church
H
8
Vogelfederberg
22° 57' 22" S
14° 31' 18" E
PERMIT
Walvis Bay Nature Reserve
24
Rooibank
Sandwich Harbour
Namib-Naukluft Park
Sandwich Harbour
R
NAMIB DESERT
KM 30
MI 15
Gobabeb Desert Research Centre (No Entry)
17
Homeb
Kuiseb
Black Cliff
Hardap

The wetlands at Sandwich Harbour offer a haven for birds, and the unspoilt coastline and spectacular scenery make it a popular tourist stop.

Four-wheel-drive trips along the Skeleton Coast offer a unique driving experience, yet demand caution and a large degree of consideration for the environment.

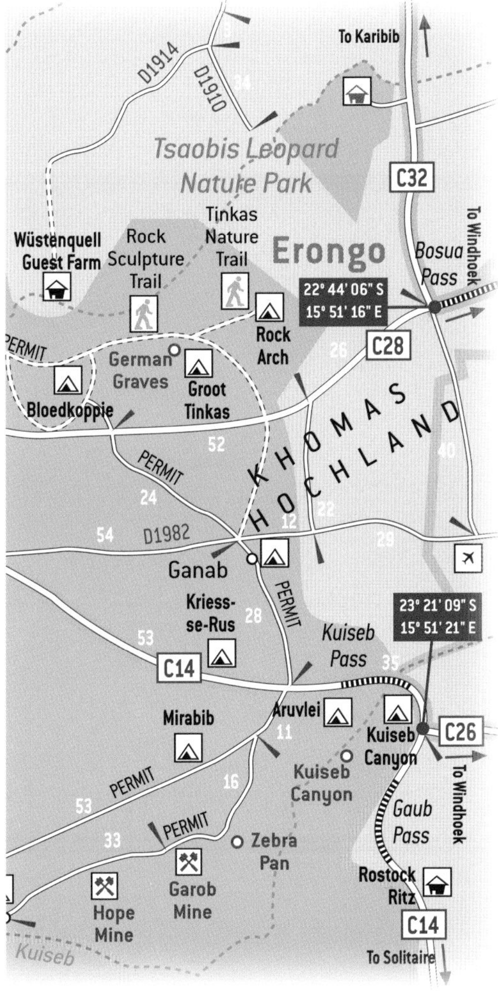

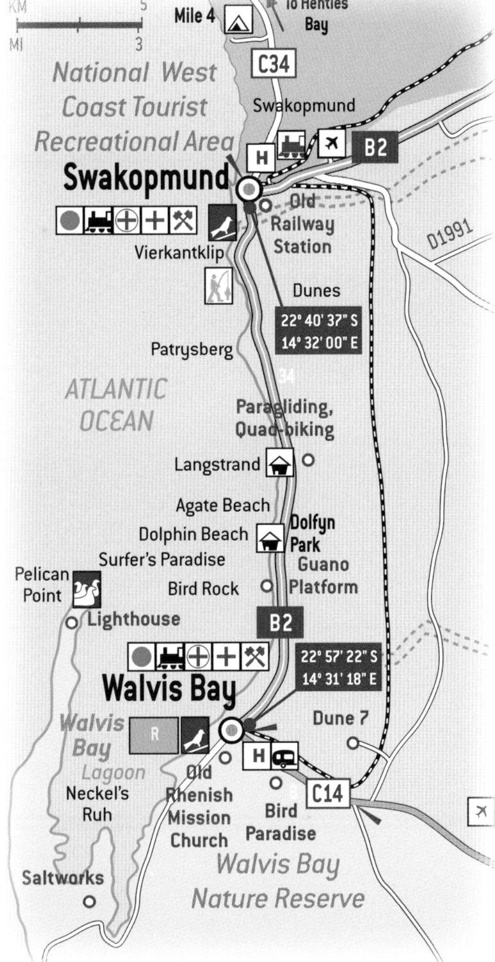

Driving in two-vehicle (at least) convoys in Nkasa Rupara (Mamili) National Park is strongly advised ... regardless of your perceived survival skills.

Nkasa Rupara (Mamili) National Park

The 32,000ha Nkasa Rupara (Mamili) National Park was opened at the same time as Mudumu (1990), and they act as the eastern Caprivi's only protected areas. The Linyandi Swamp is a major drawcard when the Kwando River is running full (often flooding around June), which provides lazy *mokoro* (dugout) trips to explore the forested islands, wetlands and reeded channels. Naturally, there is abundant bird life (more than 430 species) in addition to other wildlife (from elephant to lion, giraffe and hippo, along with numerous buck), despite the past ravages of poachers' weapons. *Mokoro* and 4x4 are the only way to get around Nkasa Rupara (Mamili) National Park. This is not the place to take personal risks, as help can be a long time coming. There are rangers on patrol throughout the park, but they might not cross your path in time if you've found your way into a spot of difficulty. Game-viewing is best before the rainy season, which can start as early as October. The best birding opportunities are between December and March when the migrants move in, but then the 'black cotton' clay (road) tracks could become totally inaccessible.

The African Jacana has unusually long toes which are well adapted for the wetland environments it frequents: the long toes allow it to walk and even run on floating plants without sinking.

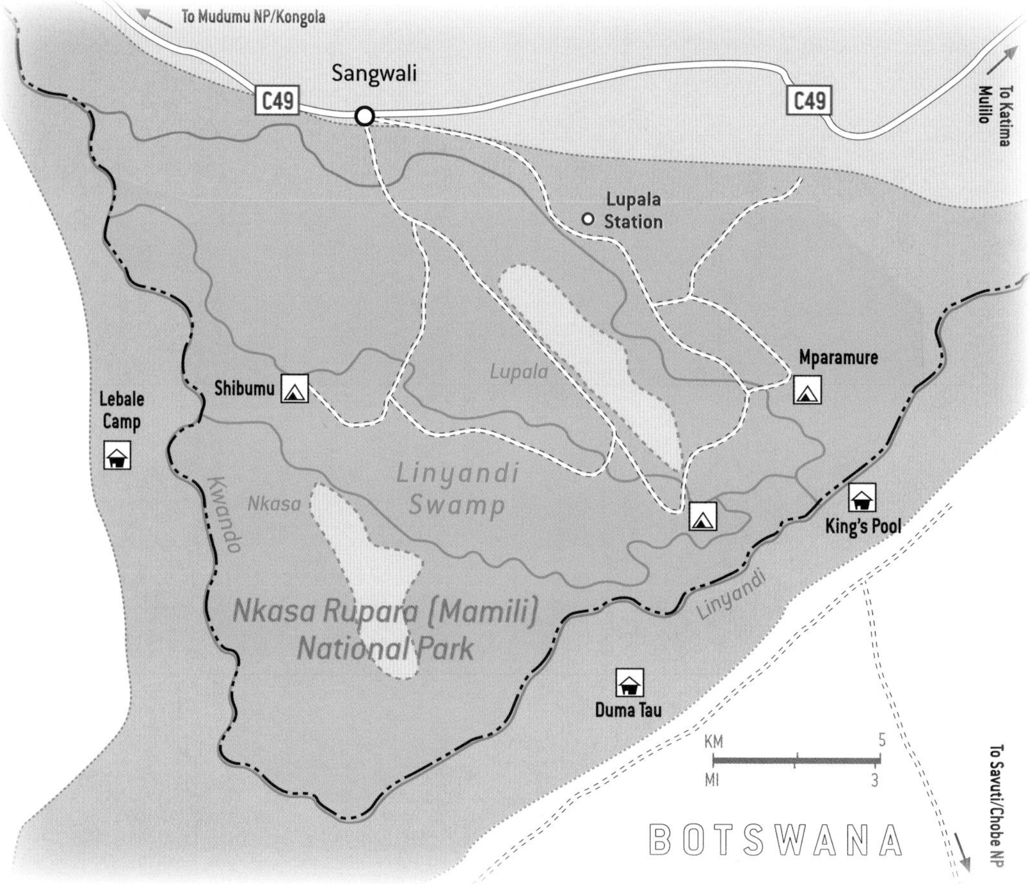

Mudumu was renowned as Namibia's greatest wildlife habitat before the ravages of poaching took their toll, but the park remains alive with fauna.

Mudumu National Park

Spread across 100,000ha, Mudumu is hugged to the west by the Kwando River, which is alive with crocodile, hippo and numerous water-loving buck (sitatunga, red lechwe and reedbuck). Covered in mopane woodlands, the reserve is well populated with elephant, giraffe and zebra, in addition to impala, kudu, red lechwe and the somewhat uncommon roan antelope species. These animals enjoy the shelter and foliage offered by the abundant mopane. Bird-watchers will fall in love with Mudumu, especially if they get to spot the African Fish Eagle, the Narina Trogon, Pel's Fishing Owl, or any of the many species found nowhere else in Namibia. It's best to explore Mudumu by 4x4, but Lianshulu Lodge and Lianshulu Bush Lodge offer guided walks. For a cultural diversion, visit the Lizauli Traditional Village just outside Mudumu to learn about traditional Caprivi lifestyles (from food to farming methods, medicine to crafts and tool-making). Lizauli is one of many local upliftment programmes and is worth supporting if you are environmentally or culturally sensitive.

Burchell's zebra enjoy the mopane-rich environment of the Mudumu National Park.

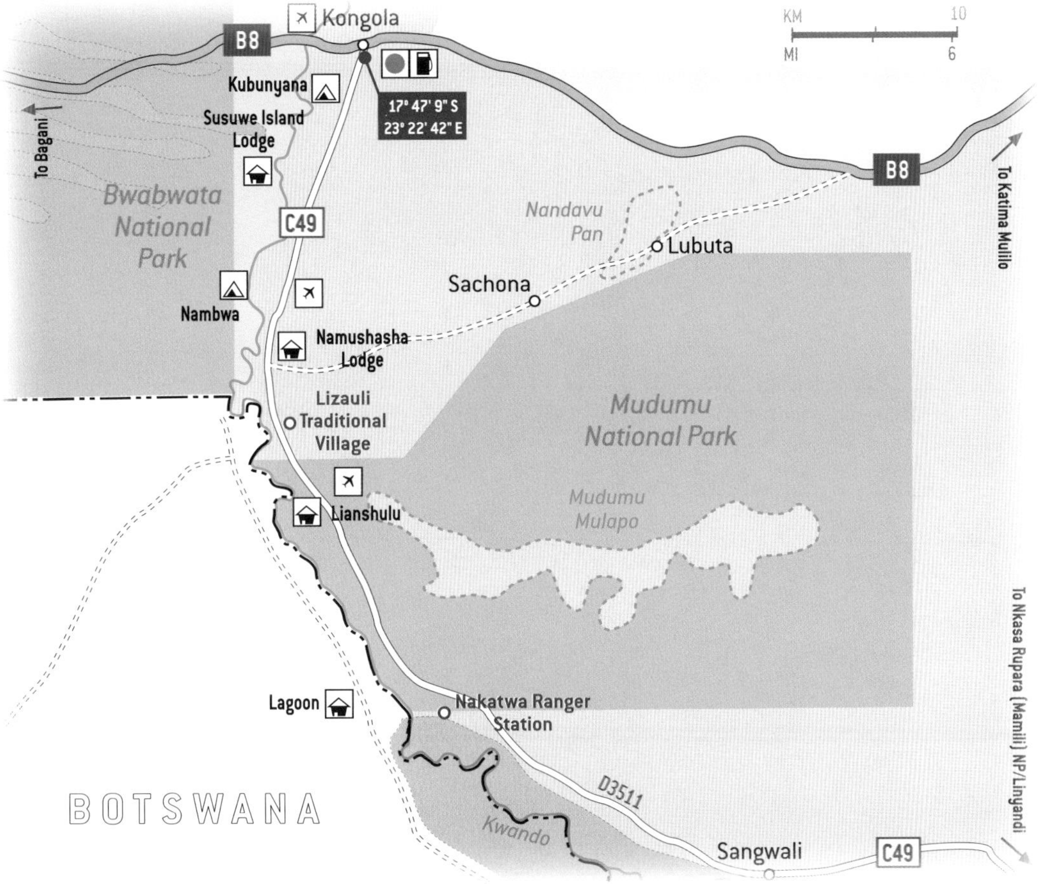

Kongola
B8
Kubunyana
Susuwe Island Lodge
17° 47' 9" S
23° 22' 42" E
To Bagani
Bwabwata National Park
C49
Nambwa
Namushasha Lodge
Lizauli Traditional Village
Lianshulu
Lagoon
Nakatwa Ranger Station
BOTSWANA
Kwando
D3511
Sangwali
C49
Nandavu Pan
Lubuta
Sachona
Mudumu National Park
Mudumu Mulapo
B8
To Katima Mulilo
To Nkasa Rupara (Mamili) NP/Linyandi
KM 10
MI 6

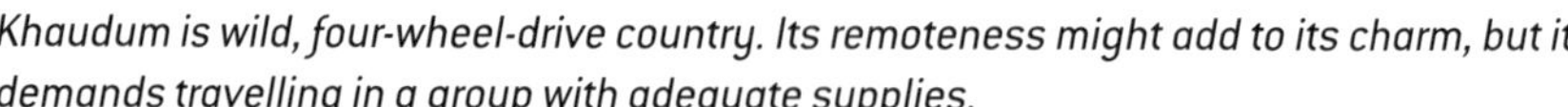

Khaudum is wild, four-wheel-drive country. Its remoteness might add to its charm, but it demands travelling in a group with adequate supplies.

Khaudum National Park

The lack of fencing around Khaudum (with the exception of the boundary with Botswana) allows animals to leave the park in search of fresh grazing and water during the rainy season, thus ensuring an abundance of wildlife to enjoy, particularly wild dogs and roan antelope. Game-viewing is best in winter, as long as you have patience and discipline: these free-roaming animals don't take kindly to noise, particularly from humans and their vehicles! The artificial water holes provide some of the best wildlife spotting. Heavier summer rain thickens the dry woodland savannah (located on settled parts of the Kalahari's sand dunes), which encourages an abundance of bird life for 'twitchers' to enjoy.

Sunset in the Khaudum National Park.

To B1
KM 15
MI 8
Kavango
18° 35' 39" S
20° 33' 45" E
Tamsu
To Kano
Cwiba
Khaudum
Khaudum
Khaudom Waterhole
Burkea Waterhole
Doringstraat Waterhole
Khaudum National Park
Tsau Waterhole
Leeupan Waterhole
BOTSWANA
Elands Drink Waterhole
Dussi Waterhole
TariKora Waterhole
Nhoma
Omuramba Waterhole
Nhoma
To Samagaigai
Soncana Waterhole
Sikereti
Baikiaea Waterhole
D3303
Sikereti Pan
To Tsumkwe

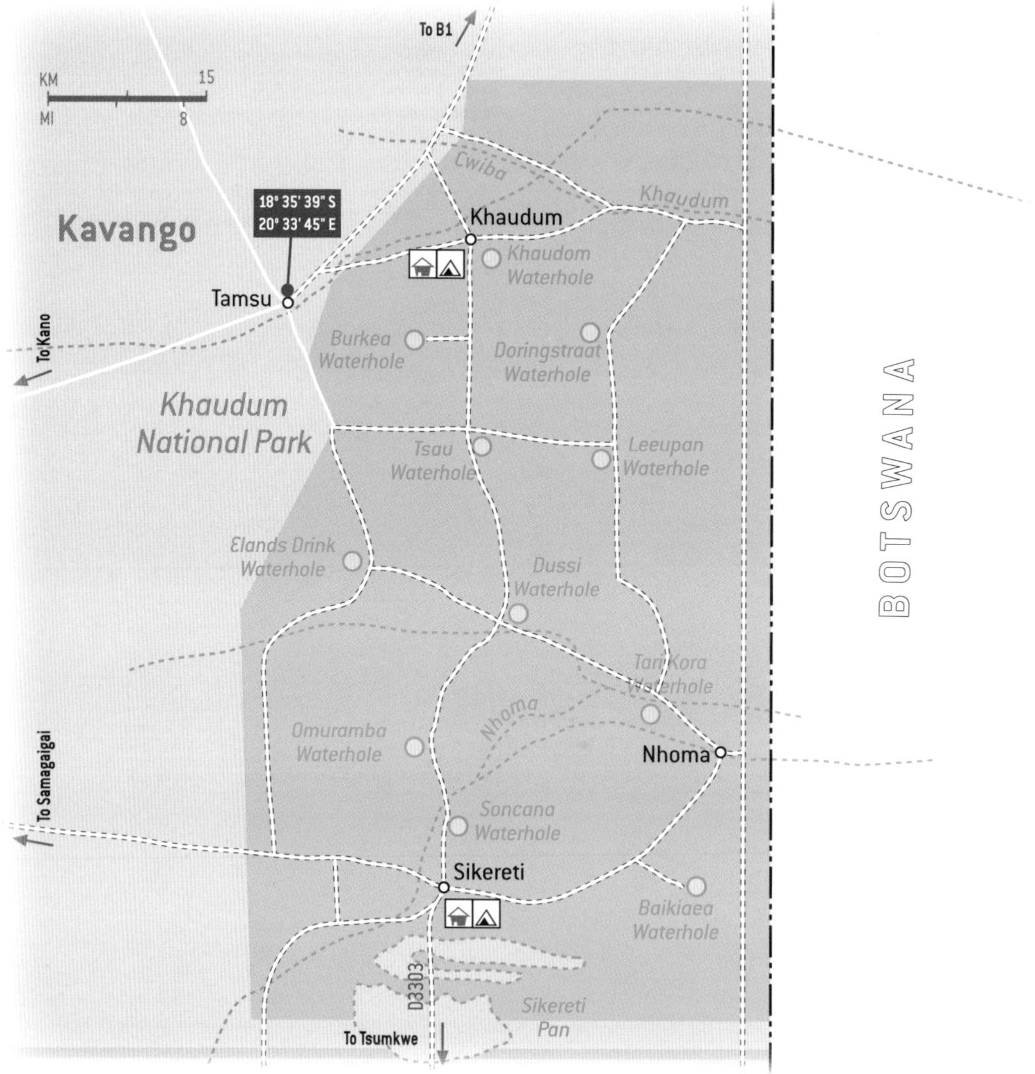

The Waterberg Plateau is centred totally on the animals and their needs. Tourists may not drive themselves around and must fit in with the animals.

Waterberg Plateau Park

The Waterberg Plateau dominates the surrounding landscape, its steep cliffs rise hundreds of metres above the surrounding plains, making the plateau a safe haven for wildlife. Many of Namibia's endangered species have been rehomed here to protect them from poachers and predators alike. This animal paradise towers a breathtaking 1800m-plus above sea level and, aided by an amazing biodiversity which enables this small park to support a wide array of animals, it is a conservation success that actually supplies rare species of game and wildlife to many of Namibia's other parks. You can drive around the park on one of the limited, organised game drive – but NOT on your own. The animals prefer it that way! Walking in the park provides incredible scenery and game-viewing opportunities. The attractions include more than 200 species of birds (with Black Eagles and Cape Vultures), as well as age-old dinosaur tracks and numerous examples of San rock art.

A natural still life in the Waterberg.

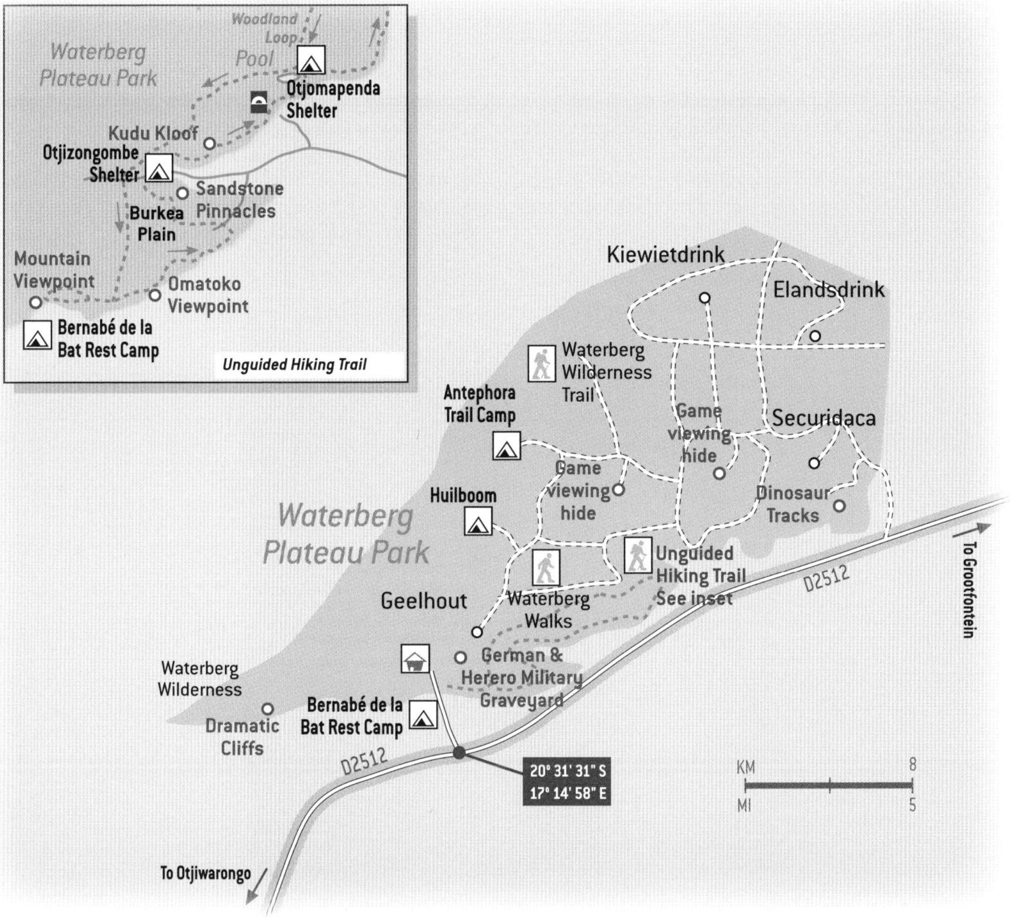

Waterberg Plateau Park
Woodland Loop
Pool
Otjomapenda Shelter
Kudu Kloof
Otjizongombe Shelter
Sandstone Pinnacles
Burkea Plain
Mountain Viewpoint
Omatoko Viewpoint
Bernabé de la Bat Rest Camp
Unguided Hiking Trail

Kiewietdrink
Elandsdrink
Waterberg Wilderness Trail
Antephora Trail Camp
Game viewing hide
Securidaca
Game viewing hide
Huilboom
Dinosaur Tracks
Waterberg Plateau Park
Unguided Hiking Trail
See inset
D2512
To Grootfontein
Geelhout
Waterberg Walks
Waterberg Wilderness
German & Herero Military Graveyard
Dramatic Cliffs
Bernabé de la Bat Rest Camp
D2512
20° 31' 31" S
17° 14' 58" E
KM 8
MI 5
To Otjiwarongo

Hardap Dam's capacity amounts to 323 million cubic metres of water held by a 39m high, 865m long dam wall, and offering a surface area of 25km^2.

Hardap, Lüderitz Peninsula

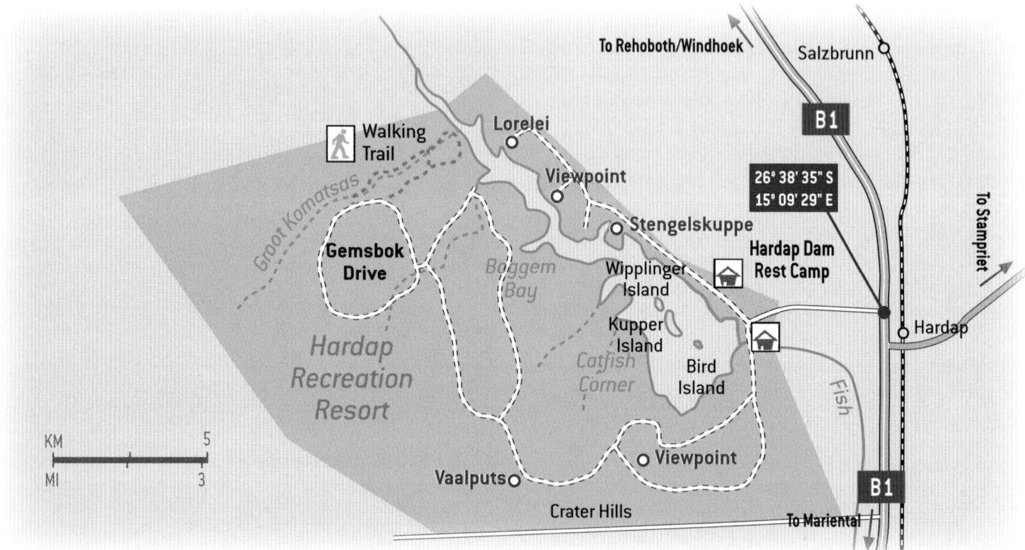

HARDAP GAME RESERVE

Hardap covers 23,420ha and offers driving trails as well as excellent predator-free walking trails, especially around Crater Hills (named for the rough terrain it encloses). The bird life is superb thanks to the large dam, with over 250 species spotted here, including the majestic African Fish Eagle.

LÜDERITZ PENINSULA

A trip around the peninsula (in calm weather) will offer up some fabulous views and swimming possibilities at one of the many bays along the coast (Dias Point and Griffith Bay offer stunning views), while the rusted remnants of Sturmvogel Bucht's 'deceased' Norwegian Whaling Station is worth a look.

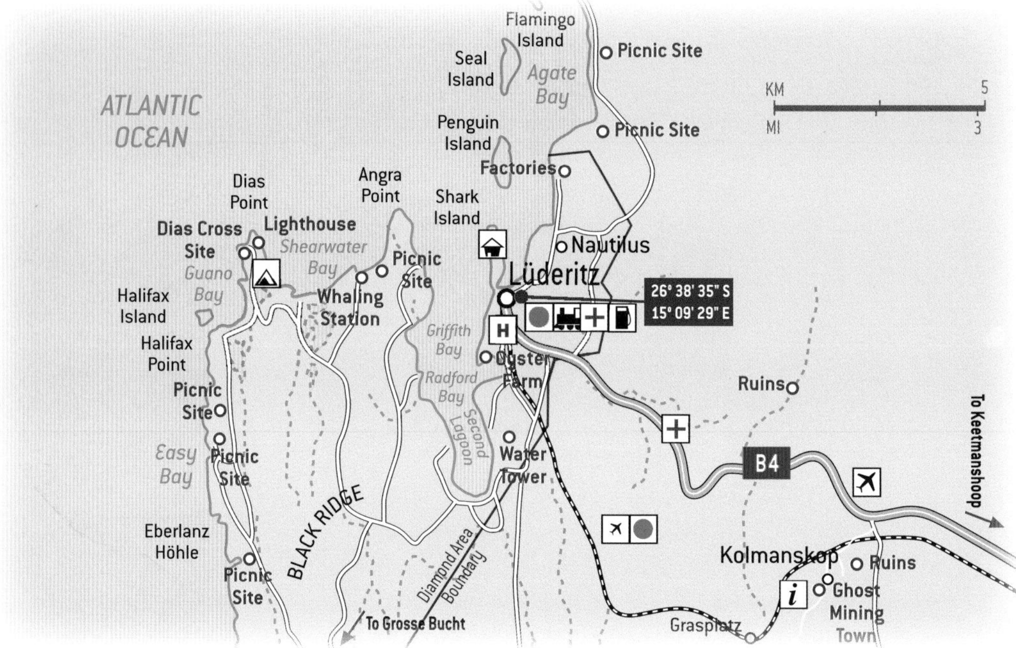

Most of Kolmanskop's buildings remain as they were 40 years ago when its inhabitants left, leaving the desert sand to invade.

Kolmanskop

The ghostly interior of a Kolmanskop house.

The desert ghost town of Kolmanskop is accessible for visitors, lying just 10km from Lüderitz. The diamond boom saw this town spring up in 1908 and become the centre of the region's diamond industry. During its boom years the streets and businesses bustled with determined prospectors, stars in their eyes, readily diving into the desert's sands in search of their fortunes. Its attraction now is as a tourist stop to explore the sand-ravaged ghost town, 'dead' for over 40 years – so you won't be able to enjoy the town's former facilities of an ice factory, casino and excellent theatre, although the skittle alley has been restored to working order.

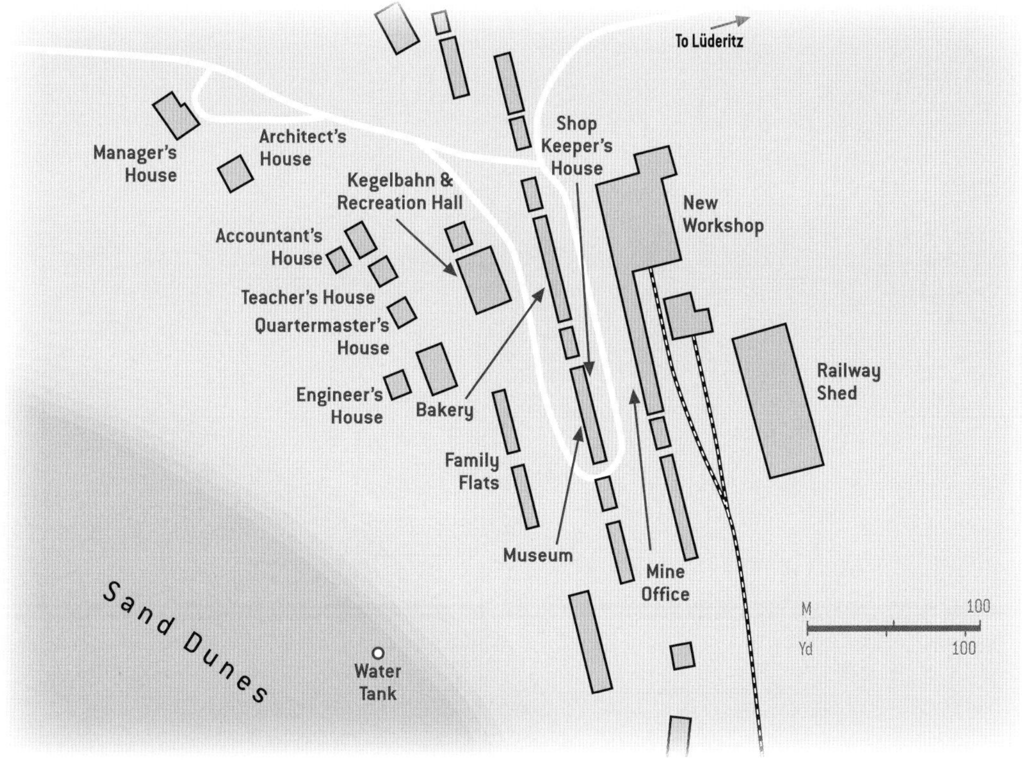

Touring/Driving Maps

Namibia's long, straight roads demand from travellers time, patience and endurance as they draw you vast distances between the country's many cultural attractions, which range from colonial outposts and strongholds through to the many traditional villages that dot the landscape. The road will also lead you through and into Namibia's many varied wilderness areas, game reserves and national parks, offering vast openness, scores of animals roaming free and great deserts untrappable by man.

A standard vehicle will take you across Namibia's 5200km of tarred roads, but a four-wheel-drive vehicle is essential if you want to explore the true depths of Namibia's 35,000km of gravel roads and other uncharted territory. However, even these hardy vehicles can fall prey to the dunes, rocky terrain and sporadic quicksand that await you once you veer off the beaten track. Trying to cut corners or pushing too hard to reach your destination on schedule is your best way to get into the sort of trouble that could dig a hole in your pocket, or worse!

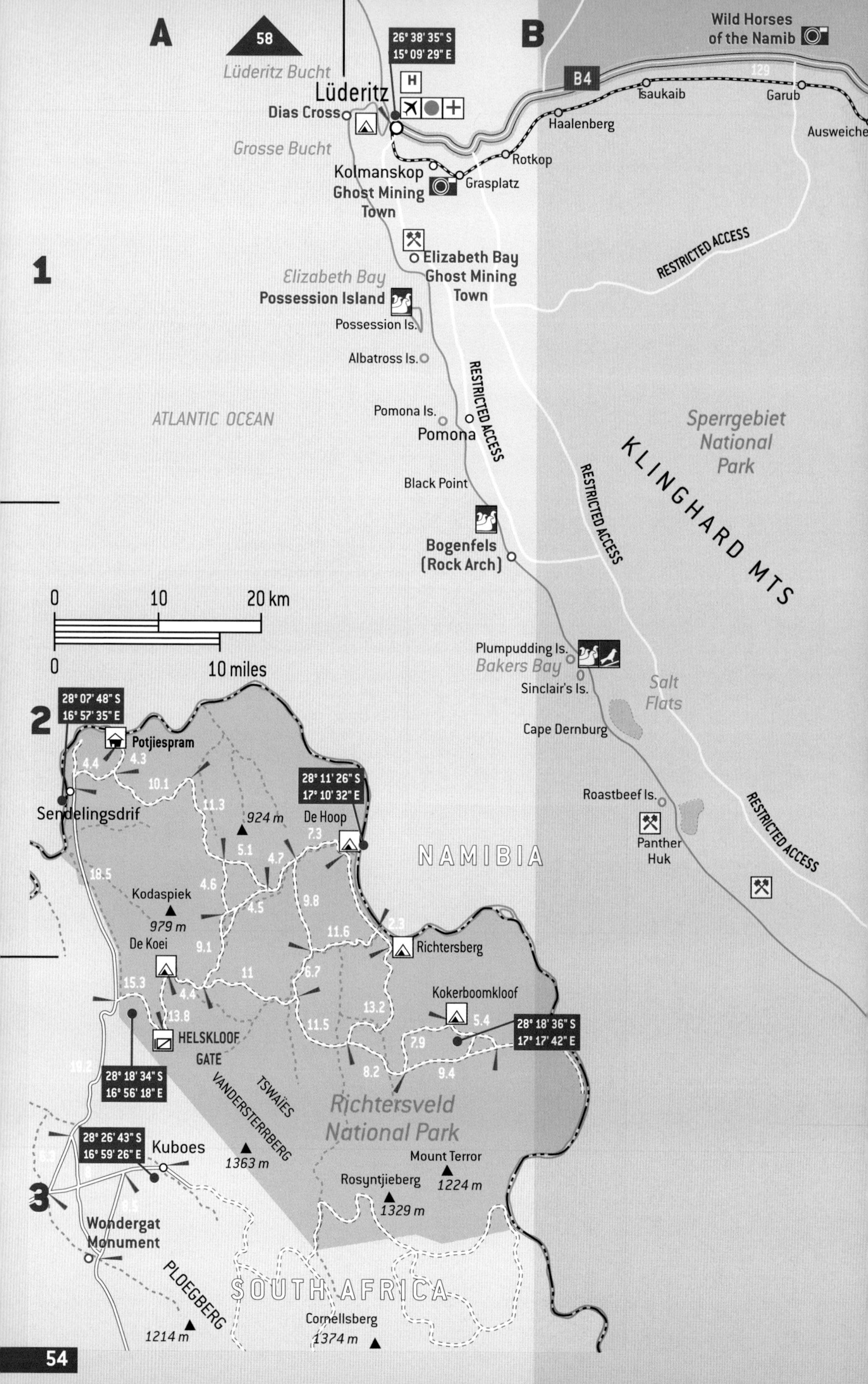
A
B
1
2
3
58
26° 38' 35" S
15° 09' 29" E
Wild Horses of the Namib
B4
129
Lüderitz Bucht
Lüderitz
Dias Cross
Grosse Bucht
Isaukaib
Garub
Ausweiche
Haalenberg
Rotkop
Grasplatz
Kolmanskop Ghost Mining Town
Elizabeth Bay Ghost Mining Town
Elizabeth Bay
Possession Island
Possession Is.
Albatross Is.
RESTRICTED ACCESS
ATLANTIC OCEAN
Pomona Is.
Pomona
Black Point
Sperrgebiet National Park
KLINGHARD MTS
Bogenfels (Rock Arch)
0
10
20 km
10 miles
Plumpudding Is.
Bakers Bay
Sinclair's Is.
Salt Flats
Cape Dernburg
Roastbeef Is.
Panther Huk
28° 07' 48" S
16° 57' 35" E
Potjiespram
Sendelingsdrif
28° 11' 26" S
17° 10' 32" E
De Hoop
924 m
NAMIBIA
Kodaspiek
979 m
De Koei
Richtersberg
Kokerboomkloof
28° 18' 36" S
17° 17' 42" E
HELSKLOOF GATE
28° 18' 34" S
16° 56' 18" E
TSWAÏES
VANDERSTERRBERG
Richtersveld National Park
28° 26' 43" S
16° 59' 26" E
Kuboes
1363 m
Mount Terror
1224 m
Rosyntjieberg
1329 m
Wondergat Monument
PLOEGBERG
SOUTH AFRICA
Cornellsberg
1374 m
1214 m
4.4
4.3
10.1
11.3
7.3
5.1
4.7
18.5
4.6
4.5
9.8
2.3
11.6
9.1
11
6.7
15.3
4.4
13.8
11.5
13.2
5.4
7.9
8.2
9.4
19.2
6.3
8
8.5

Wild Horses of the Namib
C
D
C13
59
B4
B4
Tsaukaib
Garub
Ausweiche
Aus
Ausnek
Asbospan
Guibes
Goageb
D435
D446
26° 39' 47" S
16° 15' 49" E
26° 45' 19" S
17° 13' 40" E
Klein-Aus Vista
HUIB-HOCH PLATEAU
Aukam
1700m
RESTRICTED ACCESS
C13
D727
Sperrgebiet National Park
RESTRICTED ACCESS
KLINGHARD MTS
56
Witpütz
D463
C13
Salt Flats
ǀAi-ǀAis / Richtersveld Transfrontier Park
Rosh Pinah
27° 57' 37" S
16° 45' 15" E
Roastbeef Is.
Panther Huk
RESTRICTED ACCESS
NAMIBIA
Ferry Crossing
Orange
(Gariep)
Sendelingsdrif
Richtersveld National Park
(SEE ENLARGED MAP ON PAGE 54)
28° 33' 12" S
16° 25' 57" E
NO ENTRY
Oranjemund
Oranjemund
R
Alexander Bay
Khubus
SOUTH AFRICA
Holgat
Wreck Point

Keetmanshoop
Quiver Tree Rest Camp
Historic Buildings
Gobas
Coenbult
Jurgen
Old Fort
Seeheim
Sandverhaar
Feldschuhhorn
Naute
Naute Recreation Area
Gawagab
Karas
Inachab
Huns
Holoog
1559m
Cañon Roadhouse
Fish River Canyon
Viewpoint
Cañon Lodge
Fish River Canyon Conservation Area
Gorges
Klein-Karas
Signalberg
Grünau
Narubis
2202m
GROOT KARASBERGE
Nanzes
Kanus
Satco
Karasburg
Wolplaas
Fish River Canyon Hiking Trail
Hot Springs
|Ai-|Ais
Richtersveld National Park
Orange (Gariep)
Aussenkehr
Noordoewer
Vioolsdrif
NOORDOEWER
Warmbad
Hot Springs
Goodhouse
SOUTH AFRICA
Löwen
Hom
Haib
26° 47' 53" S 17° 48' 45" E
27° 43' 26" S 18° 22' 40" E
28° 01' 10" S 18° 45' 15" E
27° 56' 30" S 18° 10' 39" E
28° 45' 03" S 17° 37' 15" E
B1
B3
B4
C10
C11
C12
C13
C16
C21
C37
N7
M22
M26
D432
D463
D545
D578
D598
D601
D607
D608
D201
D203
D206
D207
D208
D210
D211
D213
D259
D260
D270
D292
D298
D316
A
B
1
2
3
55
60

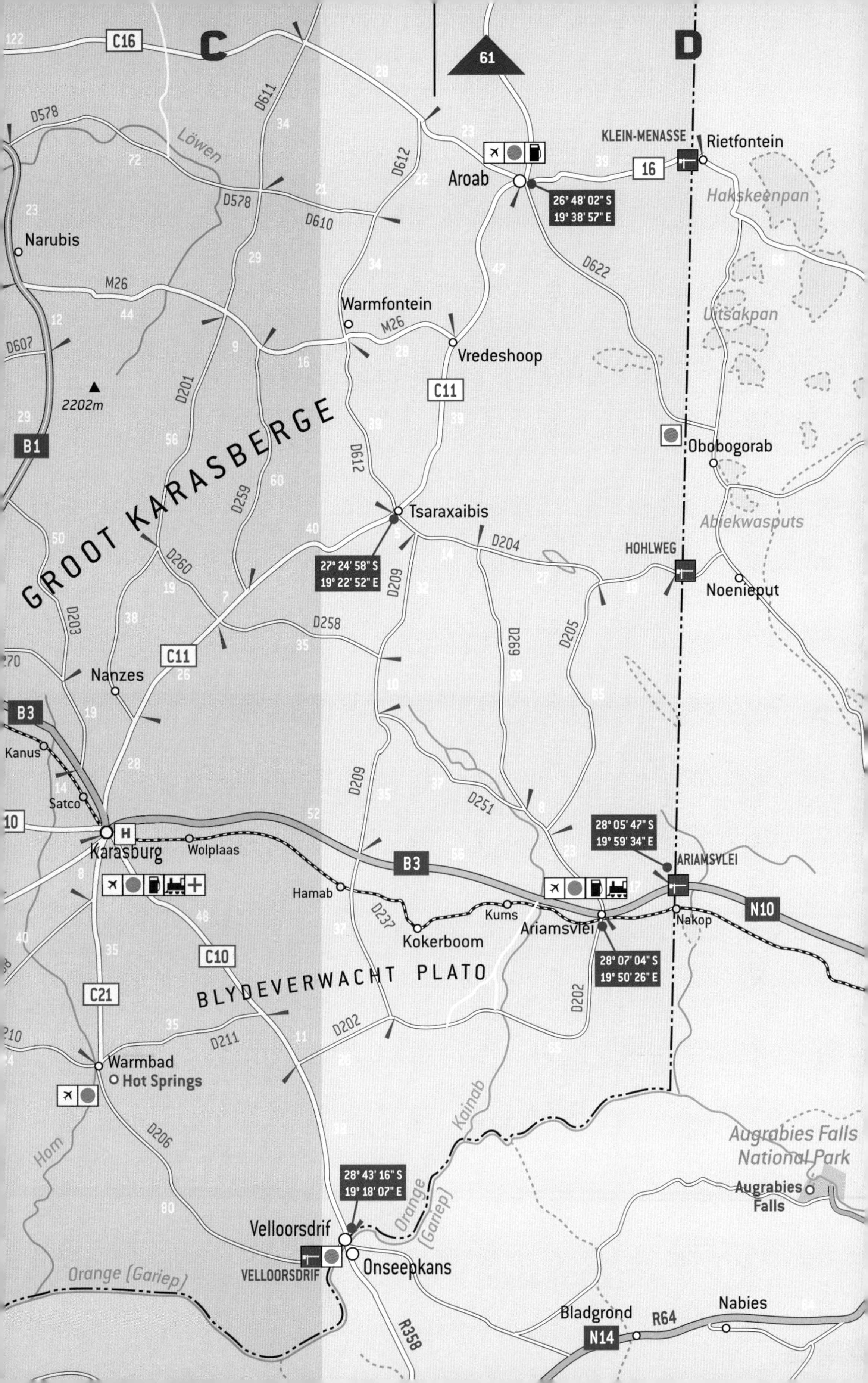

C
D
61
C16
16
Aroab
KLEIN-MENASSE
Rietfontein
26° 48' 02" S
19° 38' 57" E
Hakskeenpan
Uitsakpan
Löwen
D578
D611
D612
D610
D622
Narubis
M26
Warmfontein
Vredeshoop
D607
C11
2202m
B1
GROOT KARASBERGE
Obobogorab
Abiekwasputs
Tsaraxaibis
27° 24' 58" S
19° 22' 52" E
D201
D259
D260
D203
D204
D209
D258
D269
D205
HOHLWEG
Noenieput
Nanzes
B3
Kanus
Satco
Karasburg
Wolplaas
D251
28° 05' 47" S
19° 59' 34" E
ARIAMSVLEI
Hamab
D237
Kums
Kokerboom
Ariamsvlei
Nakop
N10
28° 07' 04" S
19° 50' 26" E
C10
C21
BLYDEVERWACHT PLATO
D202
D211
Warmbad
Hot Springs
D206
Hom
Kainab
Augrabies Falls National Park
Augrabies Falls
28° 43' 16" S
19° 18' 07" E
Velloorsdrif
VELLOORSDRIF
Onseepkans
Orange (Gariep)
R358
Bladgrond
R64
N14
Nabies

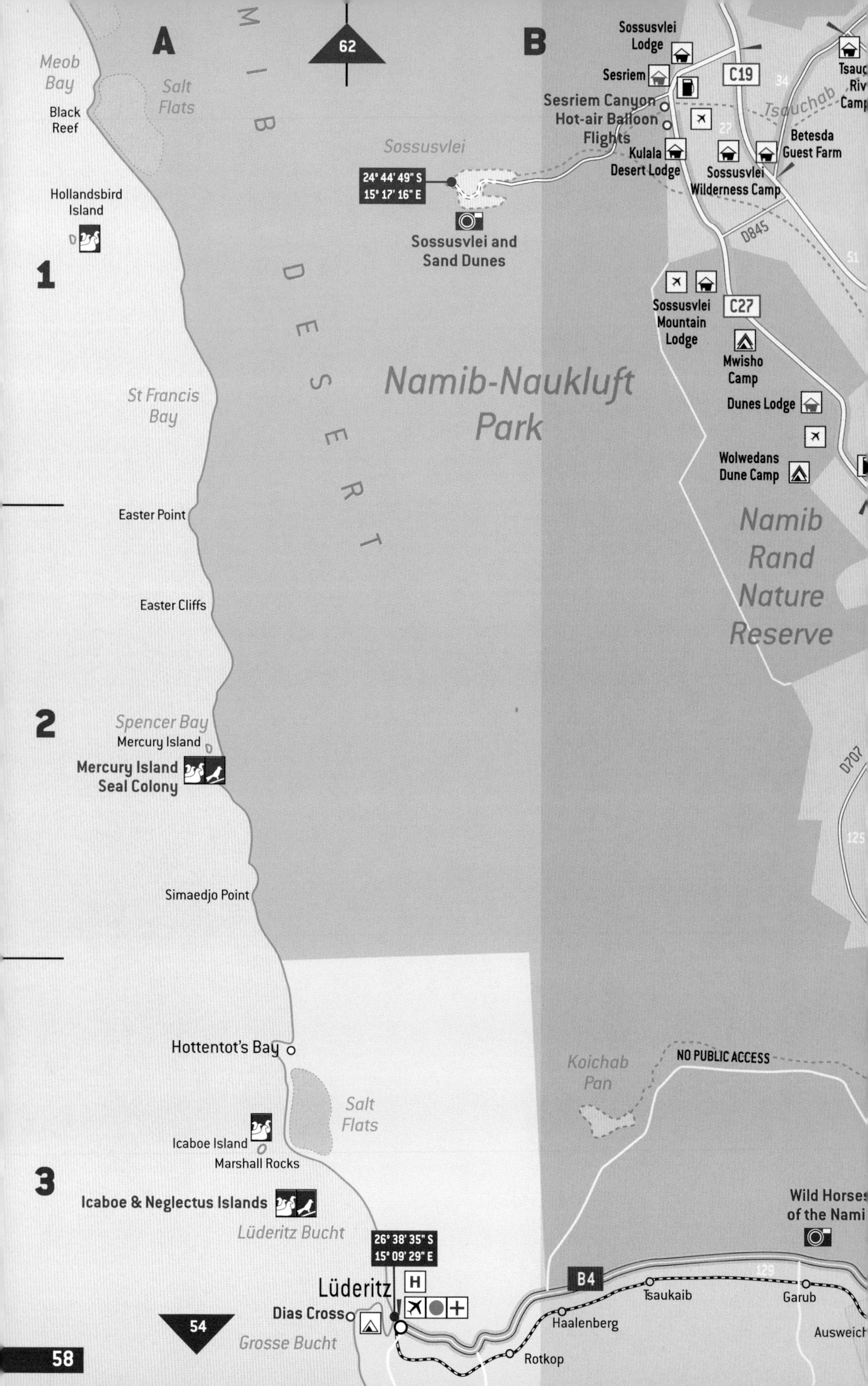
A
B
62
Meob Bay
Black Reef
Salt Flats
NAMIB DESERT
Sossusvlei
24° 44' 49" S
15° 17' 16" E
Sossusvlei and Sand Dunes
Hollandsbird Island
1
Sossusvlei Lodge
Sesriem
C19
Sesriem Canyon
Hot-air Balloon Flights
Kulala Desert Lodge
Sossusvlei Wilderness Camp
Betesda Guest Farm
Tsauchab
D845
Sossusvlei Mountain Lodge
C27
Mwisho Camp
Dunes Lodge
Wolwedans Dune Camp
Namib-Naukluft Park
Namib Rand Nature Reserve
St Francis Bay
Easter Point
Easter Cliffs
2
Spencer Bay
Mercury Island
Mercury Island Seal Colony
Simaedjo Point
D707
Hottentot's Bay
Salt Flats
Koichab Pan
NO PUBLIC ACCESS
Icaboe Island
Marshall Rocks
3
Icaboe & Neglectus Islands
Lüderitz Bucht
26° 38' 35" S
15° 09' 29" E
Lüderitz
Dias Cross
Grosse Bucht
54
B4
Tsaukaib
Garub
Haalenberg
Rotkop
Wild Horses of the Nami

C
D
63
60
55
Sossusvlei Lodge
Sesriem
Sesriem Canyon
Hot-air Balloon Flights
Kulala Desert Lodge
Sossusvlei Wilderness Camp
Betesda Guest Farm
Tsauchab River Camping
Tsauchab
Zebra River Lodge
Fish
Nomtsas
C19
C21
C14
C27
C13
B4
D855
D850
D861
D831
D845
D827
D830
D826
D808
D811
D813
D1089
D804
D707
D414
D421
D425
D437
D435
D446
TSARISBERGE
1895m
24° 57' 23" S 16° 20' 34" E
24° 52' 40" S 16° 33' 19" E
24° 49' 38" S 17° 06' 53" E
Namseb Game Lodge
Maltahöhe
Zaris
Zarishoogte Pass
Grootfontein
Sossusvlei Mountain Lodge
Mwisho Camp
Dunes Lodge
Wolwedans Dune Camp
25° 15' 42" S 16° 32' 34" E
Duwisib Castle
Hudup
SCHWARZRAND
Huams
25° 12' 35" S 16° 09' 47" E
25° 23' 14" S 16° 25' 21" E
25° 32' 25" S 16° 19' 16" E
Namib Rand Nature Reserve
ROOIRAND
1920m
Sinclair Guest Farm
Namib-Naukluft Park
25° 53' 26" S 16° 49' 13" E
Helmeringhausen
Mooifontein
Mooifontein Military Cemetery
Great Tiras
1867m
Neisip
View of Neisip Plains
Konkiep
House Schmelen
Bethanie
Koichab Pan
NO PUBLIC ACCESS
Wild Horses of the Namib
26° 39' 47" S 16° 15' 49" E
Tsaukaib
Garub
Ausweiche
Aus
Ausnek
Klein-Aus Vista
Asbospan
Guibes
Rosenberg

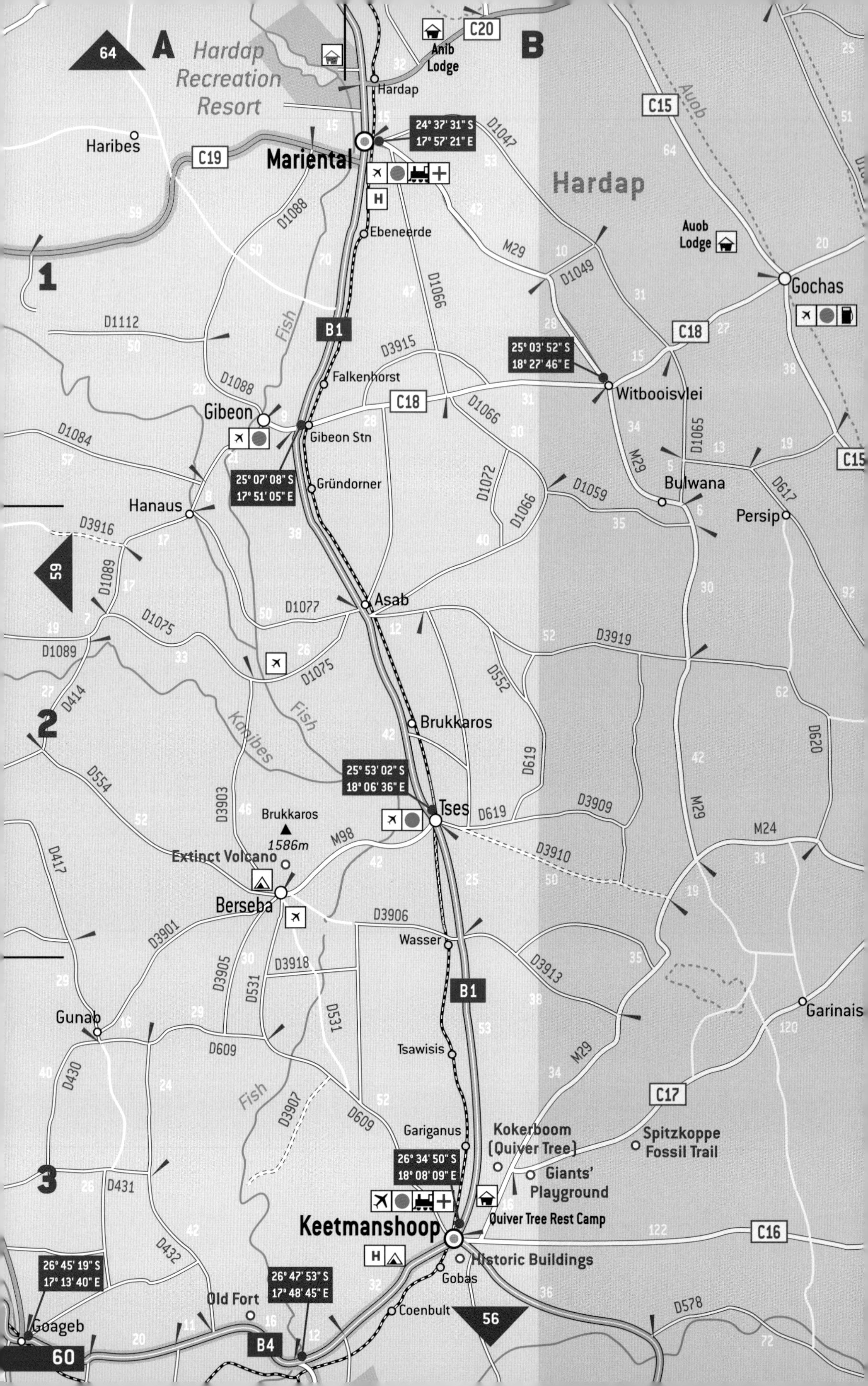

64
A
B
Hardap Recreation Resort
Anib Lodge
C20
Hardap
Haribes
C19
Mariental
24° 37' 31" S 17° 57' 21" E
D1047
C15
Auob
Hardap
D1088
Ebeneerde
M29
D1049
Auob Lodge
Gochas
1
D1066
Fish
D1112
B1
D3915
25° 03' 52" S 18° 27' 46" E
C18
Falkenhorst
Witbooisvlei
Gibeon
Gibeon Stn
D1084
D1065
M29
Bulwana
D617
C15
Gründorner
25° 07' 08" S 17° 51' 05" E
D1072
D1059
Hanaus
Persip
D3916
59
D1089
Asab
D1077
D1075
D3919
D1089
D552
D414
Kanibes
Fish
2
Brukkaros
D620
D554
25° 53' 02" S 18° 06' 36" E
D619
D3909
M29
D3903
Tses
D619
Brukkaros
1586m
M98
M24
D417
Extinct Volcano
D3910
Berseba
D3906
D3901
Wasser
D3913
D3905
D531
D3918
B1
Garinais
Gunab
D531
D609
Tsawisis
M29
D430
Fish
D3907
D609
C17
Gariganus
Kokerboom (Quiver Tree)
Spitzkoppe Fossil Trail
26° 34' 50" S 18° 08' 09" E
Giants' Playground
3
D431
Quiver Tree Rest Camp
Keetmanshoop
C16
D432
Historic Buildings
26° 45' 19" S 17° 13' 40" E
26° 47' 53" S 17° 48' 45" E
Gobas
Old Fort
Coenbult
56
D578
Goageb
B4
60

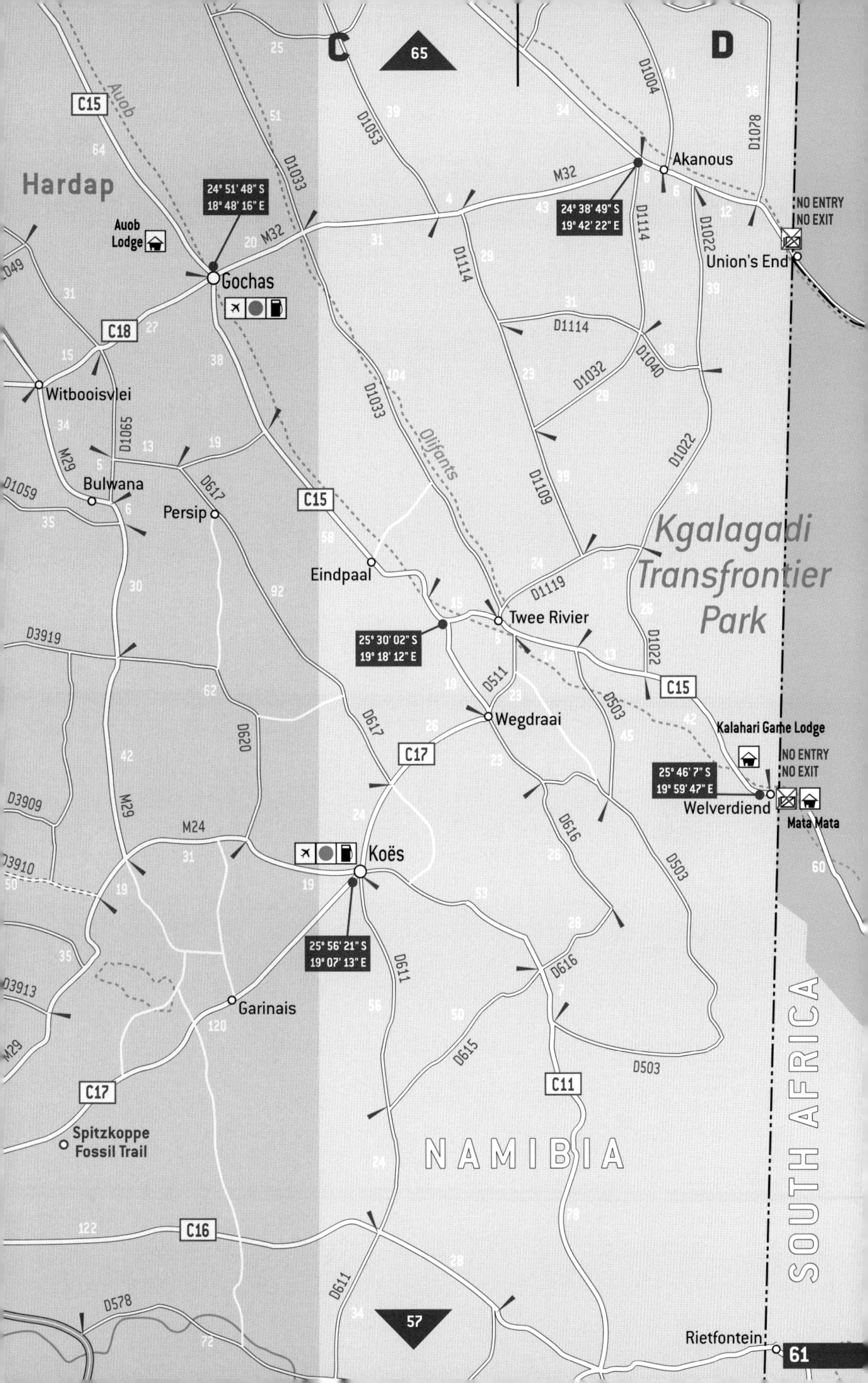

C
D
65
Hardap
Auob
Auob Lodge
Gochas
24° 51' 48" S
18° 48' 16" E
Akanous
24° 38' 49" S
19° 42' 22" E
NO ENTRY
NO EXIT
Union's End
Witbooisvlei
Bulwana
Persip
Eindpaal
Olifants
Twee Rivier
25° 30' 02" S
19° 18' 12" E
Wegdraai
Kgalagadi Transfrontier Park
Kalahari Game Lodge
25° 46' 7" S
19° 59' 47" E
Welverdiend
Mata Mata
Koës
25° 56' 21" S
19° 07' 13" E
Garinais
Spitzkoppe Fossil Trail
NAMIBIA
SOUTH AFRICA
Rietfontein
57
C15
C18
C17
C16
C11
M32
M29
M24
D1033
D1053
D1114
D1004
D1078
D1022
D1032
D1040
D1109
D1119
D1065
D617
D620
D511
D503
D616
D615
D611
D578
D3919
D3909
D3910
D3913
D1059

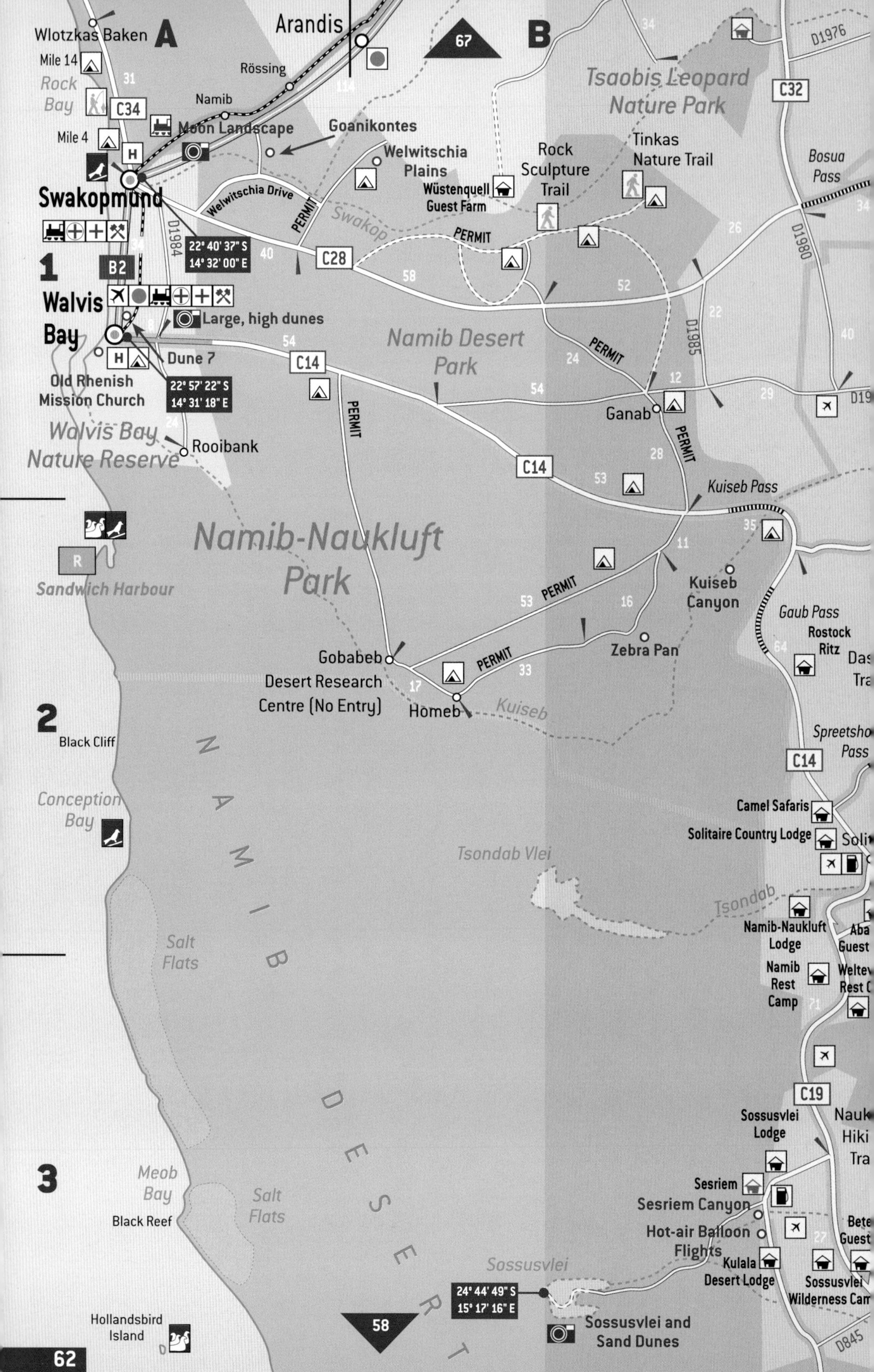

Wlotzkas Baken
A
Arandis
67
B
Mile 14
Rössing
Rock Bay
C34
Namib
Tsaobis Leopard Nature Park
C32
D1976
Mile 4
Moon Landscape
Goanikontes
Welwitschia Plains
Rock Sculpture Trail
Tinkas Nature Trail
Bosua Pass
Swakopmund
Welwitschia Drive
Wüstenquell Guest Farm
PERMIT
Swakop
D1984
22° 40' 37" S
14° 32' 00" E
C28
D1980
1
B2
Walvis Bay
Large, high dunes
Namib Desert Park
D1985
C14
Dune 7
Old Rhenish Mission Church
22° 57' 22" S
14° 31' 18" E
Ganab
Walvis Bay Nature Reserve
Rooibank
Kuiseb Pass
Namib-Naukluft Park
Sandwich Harbour
Kuiseb Canyon
Gaub Pass
Rostock Ritz
Gobabeb
Desert Research Centre (No Entry)
Zebra Pan
Homeb
Kuiseb
2
Black Cliff
Spreetshoogte Pass
Conception Bay
NAMIB DESERT
Camel Safaris
Solitaire Country Lodge
Tsondab Vlei
Tsondab
Namib-Naukluft Lodge
Namib Rest Camp
Salt Flats
C19
Sossusvlei Lodge
3
Meob Bay
Black Reef
Sesriem
Sesriem Canyon
Hot-air Balloon Flights
Kulala Desert Lodge
Sossusvlei Wilderness Camp
Sossusvlei
24° 44' 49" S
15° 17' 16" E
Sossusvlei and Sand Dunes
58
Hollandsbird Island
D845

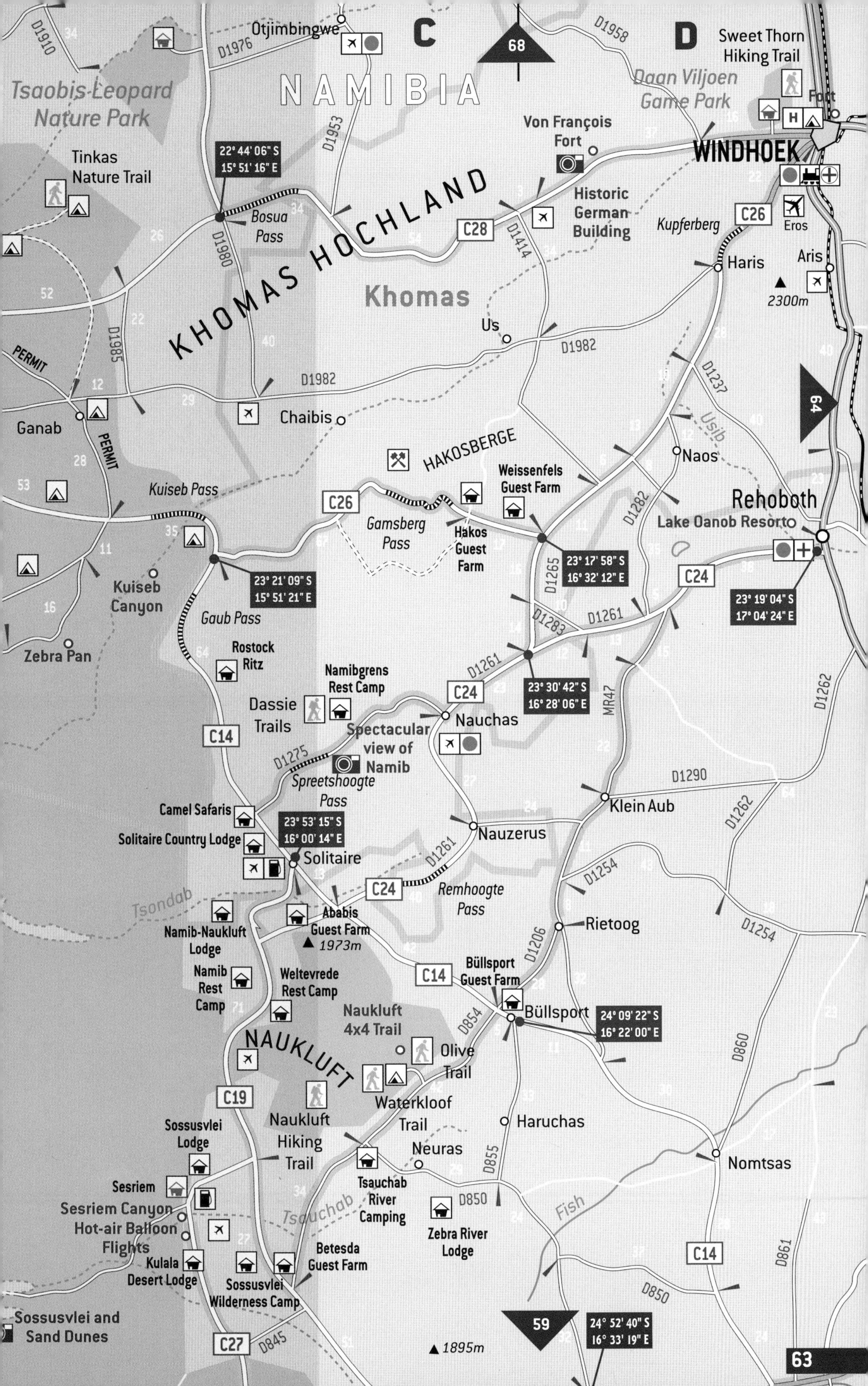
NAMIBIA
C
D
68
64
59
Otjimbingwe
D1910
D1976
D1958
D1953
Tsaobis Leopard Nature Park
Daan Viljoen Game Park
Sweet Thorn Hiking Trail
Fort
Von François Fort
WINDHOEK
22° 44' 06" S
15° 51' 16" E
Tinkas Nature Trail
KHOMAS HOCHLAND
Bosua Pass
D1980
C28
D1414
Historic German Building
Kupferberg
C26
Eros
Haris
Aris
2300m
Khomas
Us
D1982
D1985
PERMIT
Ganab
Chaibis
D1237
Usib
Naos
HAKOSBERGE
Weissenfels Guest Farm
Kuiseb Pass
C26
Gamsberg Pass
Hakos Guest Farm
D1282
Rehoboth
Lake Oanob Resort
23° 17' 58" S
16° 32' 12" E
D1265
C24
23° 21' 09" S
15° 51' 21" E
Kuiseb Canyon
Gaub Pass
D1283
D1261
23° 19' 04" S
17° 04' 24" E
Zebra Pan
Rostock Ritz
23° 30' 42" S
16° 28' 06" E
MR47
D1262
Namibgrens Rest Camp
Dassie Trails
Nauchas
C14
Spectacular view of Namib
D1275
Spreetshoogte Pass
D1290
Klein Aub
Camel Safaris
Solitaire Country Lodge
23° 53' 15" S
16° 00' 14" E
Nauzerus
Solitaire
D1254
Tsondab
C24
Remhoogte Pass
Ababis Guest Farm
Namib-Naukluft Lodge
1973m
Rietoog
D1206
Namib Rest Camp
Weltevrede Rest Camp
Büllsport Guest Farm
Naukluft 4x4 Trail
D854
Büllsport
24° 09' 22" S
16° 22' 00" E
NAUKLUFT
Olive Trail
D860
C19
Waterkloof Trail
Sossusvlei Lodge
Naukluft Hiking Trail
Haruchas
Neuras
Nomtsas
D855
Sesriem
Sesriem Canyon
Tsauchab River Camping
D850
Fish
Hot-air Balloon Flights
Tsauchab
Zebra River Lodge
Kulala Desert Lodge
Betesda Guest Farm
C14
D861
Sossusvlei Wilderness Camp
D850
Sossusvlei and Sand Dunes
C27
D845
1895m
24° 52' 40" S
16° 33' 19" E

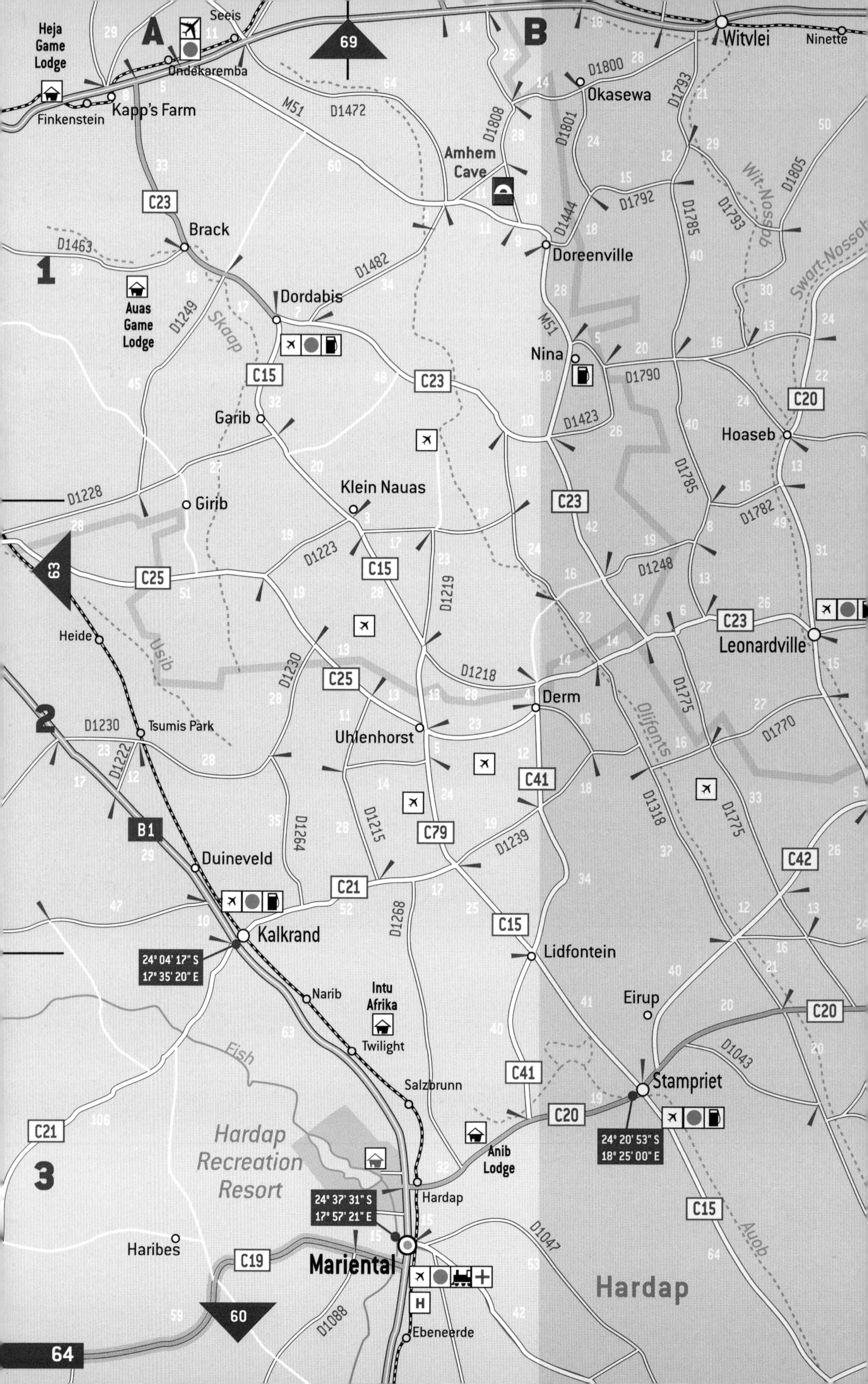
A
B
69
63
60
1
2
3
Heja Game Lodge
Seeis
Ondekaremba
Finkenstein
Kapp's Farm
M51
D1472
Witvlei
Ninette
D1800
Okasewa
D1808
D1801
D1793
Amhem Cave
C23
Brack
D1463
Auas Game Lodge
D1482
D1444
D1792
D1785
Wit-Nossob
D1805
Swart-Nossob
Doreenville
Dordabis
D1249
Skaap
C15
Nina
D1790
C20
Garib
D1423
Hoaseb
Klein Nauas
D1228
Girib
D1782
D1223
C25
D1248
D1219
Heide
Usib
D1230
Leonardville
D1218
Derm
D1775
Olifants
Tsumis Park
D1222
Uhlenhorst
D1770
C41
B1
D1215
D1264
C79
D1239
D1318
C42
Duineveld
C21
D1268
Kalkrand
24° 04' 17" S
17° 35' 20" E
Lidfontein
Narib
Intu Afrika Twilight
Eirup
Fish
D1043
Salzbrunn
Stampriet
24° 20' 53" S
18° 25' 00" E
Hardap Recreation Resort
Anib Lodge
Hardap
24° 37' 31" S
17° 57' 21" E
Auob
D1047
Haribes
C19
Mariental
H
Hardap
D1088
Ebeneerde

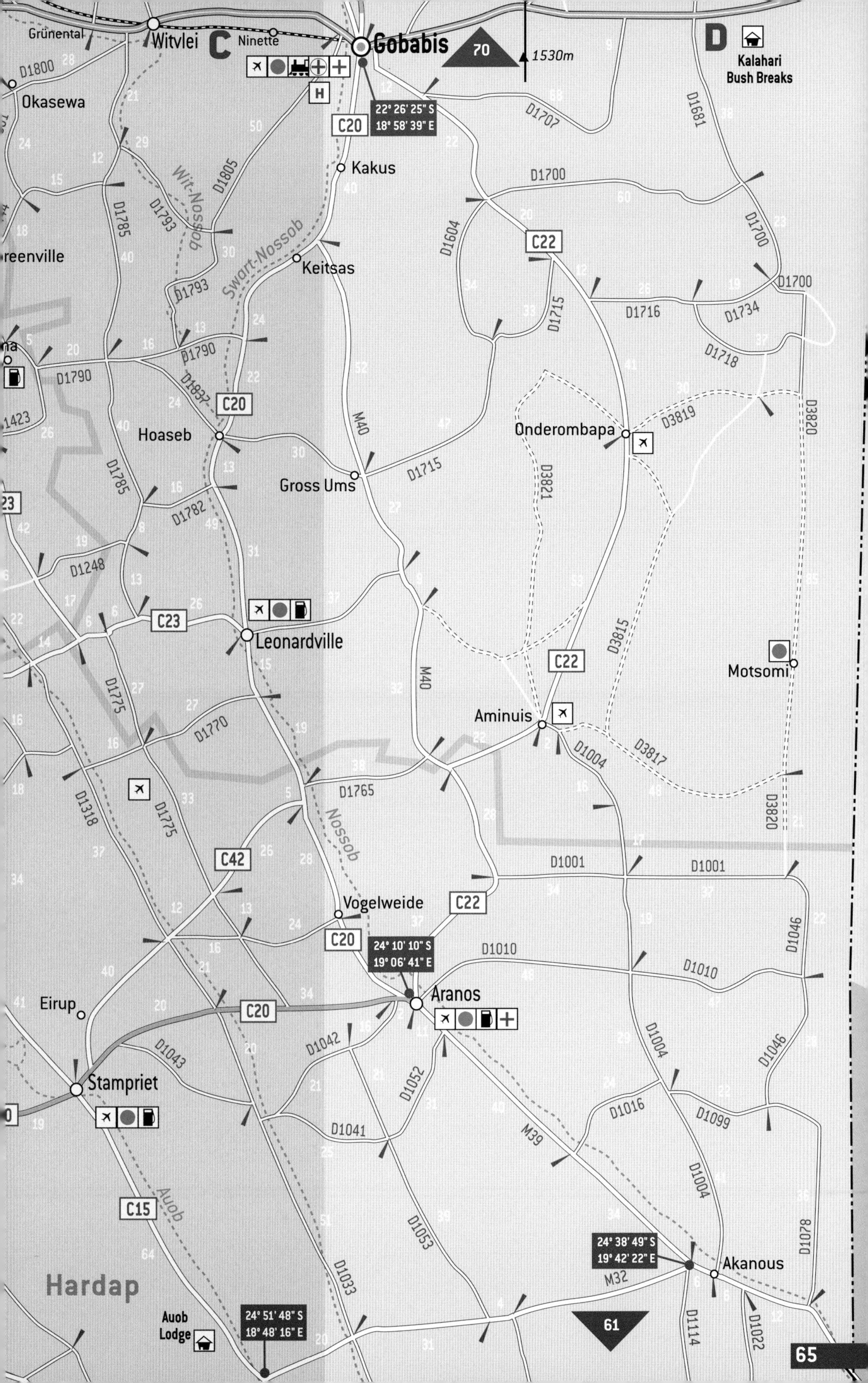
Grünental
Witvlei
C
Ninette
Gobabis
70
1530m
D
Kalahari
Bush Breaks
D1800
Okasewa
H
22° 26' 25" S
18° 58' 39" E
C20
D1707
D1681
Kakus
Wit-Nossob
D1805
D1785
D1793
D1700
D1604
C22
Swart-Nossob
Keitsas
reenville
D1793
D1716
D1734
D1700
D1715
D1790
D1718
D1790
D1837
C20
1423
Hoaseb
M40
Onderombapa
D3819
D3820
D1785
D1715
Gross Ums
D3821
D1782
D1248
D3815
C23
Leonardville
C22
Motsomi
D1775
M40
Aminuis
D1770
D1004
D3817
D1765
D1318
D1775
Nossob
D3820
C42
D1001
D1001
Vogelweide
C22
D1046
C20
24° 10' 10" S
19° 06' 41" E
D1010
D1010
Eirup
C20
Aranos
D1043
D1042
D1004
D1046
Stampriet
D1052
D1016
D1099
D1041
M39
D1004
Auob
C15
D1053
D1078
24° 38' 49" S
19° 42' 22" E
Akanous
Hardap
D1033
M32
Auob
Lodge
24° 51' 48" S
18° 48' 16" E
61
D1114
D1022

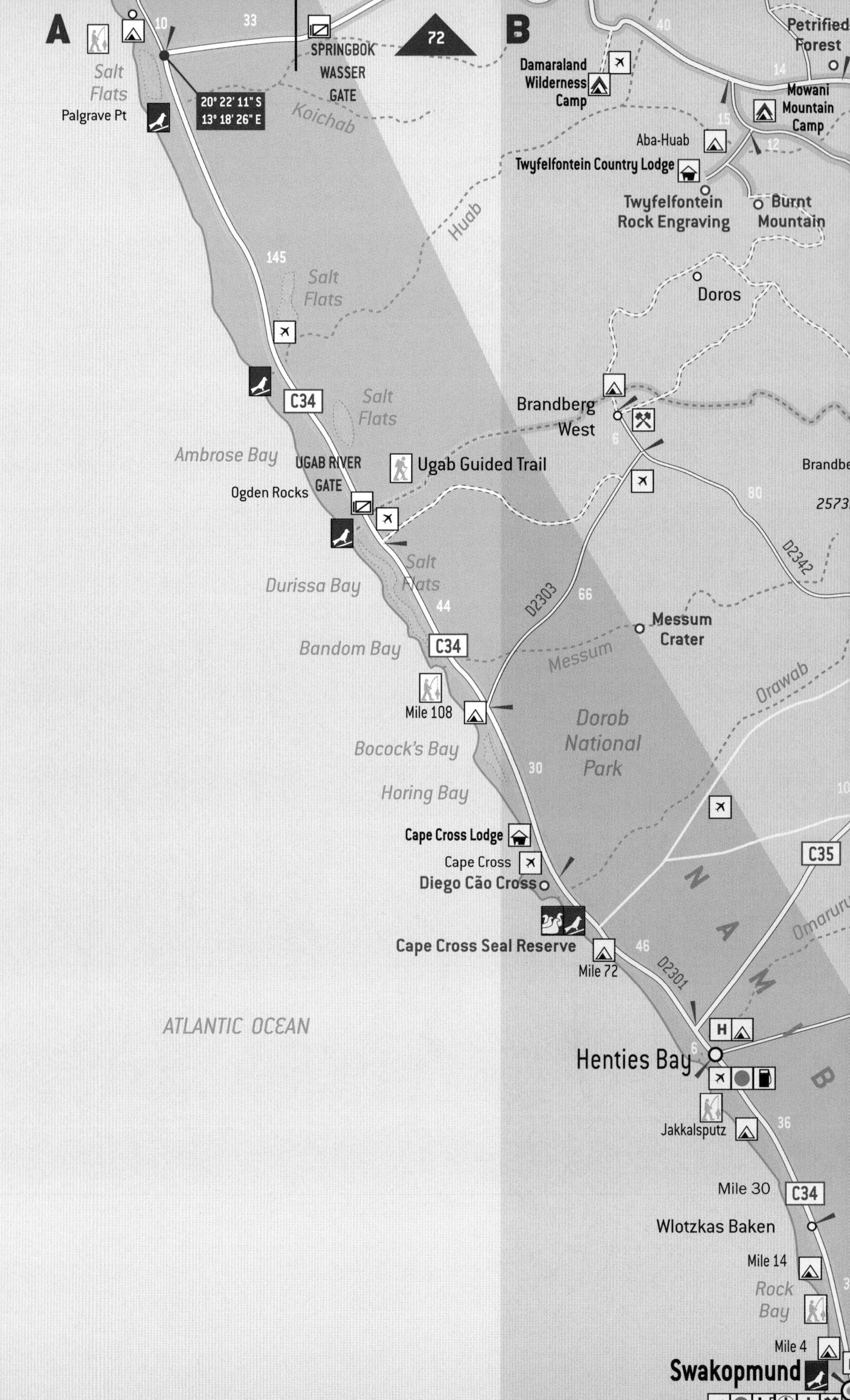
A
B
1
2
3
72
Salt Flats
Palgrave Pt
20° 22' 11" S
13° 18' 26" E
SPRINGBOK WASSER GATE
Koichab
Huab
Damaraland Wilderness Camp
Petrified Forest
Mowani Mountain Camp
Aba-Huab
Twyfelfontein Country Lodge
Twyfelfontein Rock Engraving
Burnt Mountain
Doros
Brandberg West
Brandbe
2573
D2342
C34
Ambrose Bay
UGAB RIVER GATE
Ogden Rocks
Ugab Guided Trail
Durissa Bay
Bandom Bay
Mile 108
D2303
Messum Crater
Messum
Orawab
Dorob National Park
Bocock's Bay
Horing Bay
Cape Cross Lodge
Cape Cross
Diego Cão Cross
Cape Cross Seal Reserve
Mile 72
D2301
C35
Omaruru
NAMIB
ATLANTIC OCEAN
Henties Bay
Jakkalsputz
Mile 30
Wlotzkas Baken
Mile 14
Rock Bay
Mile 4
Swakopmund

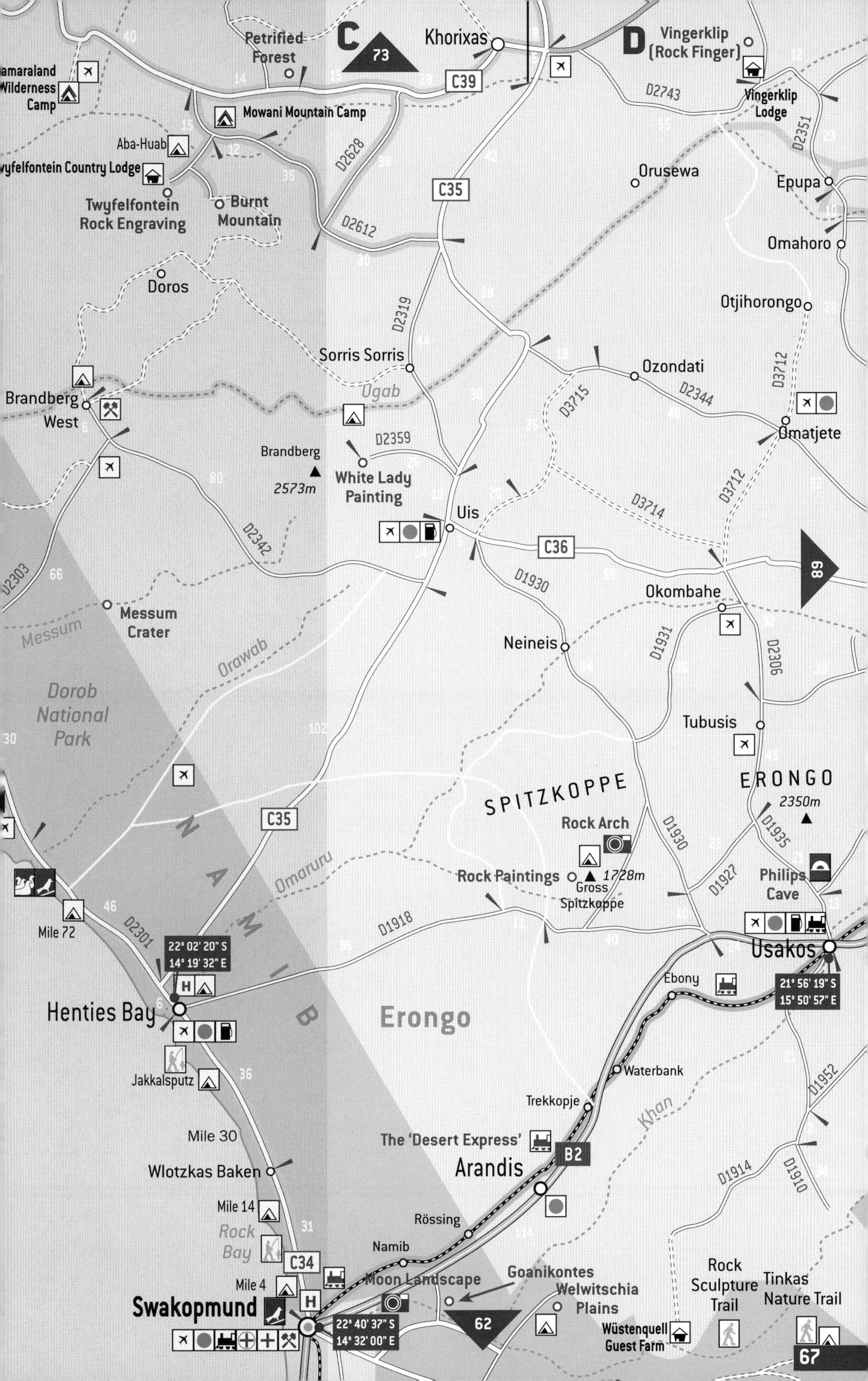

C
73
Khorixas
D
Vingerklip
(Rock Finger)
Damaraland
Wilderness
Camp
Petrified
Forest
C39
Mowani Mountain Camp
Vingerklip
Lodge
D2743
D2351
Aba-Huab
Twyfelfontein Country Lodge
Twyfelfontein
Rock Engraving
Burnt
Mountain
D2628
C35
Orusewa
Epupa
D2612
Omahoro
Doros
D2319
Otjihorongo
Sorris Sorris
Ozondati
D3712
Brandberg
West
Ogab
D3715
D2344
D2359
Omatjete
Brandberg
2573m
White Lady
Painting
D3712
Uis
D3714
D2342
C36
89
D2303
D1930
Okombahe
Messum
Crater
Messum
Neineis
D1931
D2306
Orawab
Dorob
National
Park
Tubusis
SPITZKOPPE
ERONGO
2350m
Rock Arch
C35
N
A
M
I
B
D1930
D1935
Omaruru
Rock Paintings
1728m
Gross
Spitzkoppe
D1927
Philips
Cave
Mile 72
D2301
D1918
22° 02' 20" S
14° 19' 32" E
Usakos
H
Ebony
Henties Bay
21° 56' 19" S
15° 50' 57" E
Erongo
Jakkalsputz
Waterbank
D1952
Trekkopje
Khan
Mile 30
The 'Desert Express'
B2
Wlotzkas Baken
Arandis
D1914
D1910
Mile 14
Rössing
Rock
Bay
C34
Namib
Rock
Sculpture
Trail
Tinkas
Nature Trail
Mile 4
Moon Landscape
Goanikontes
Welwitschia
Plains
Swakopmund
H
62
Wüstenquell
Guest Farm
22° 40' 37" S
14° 32' 00" E

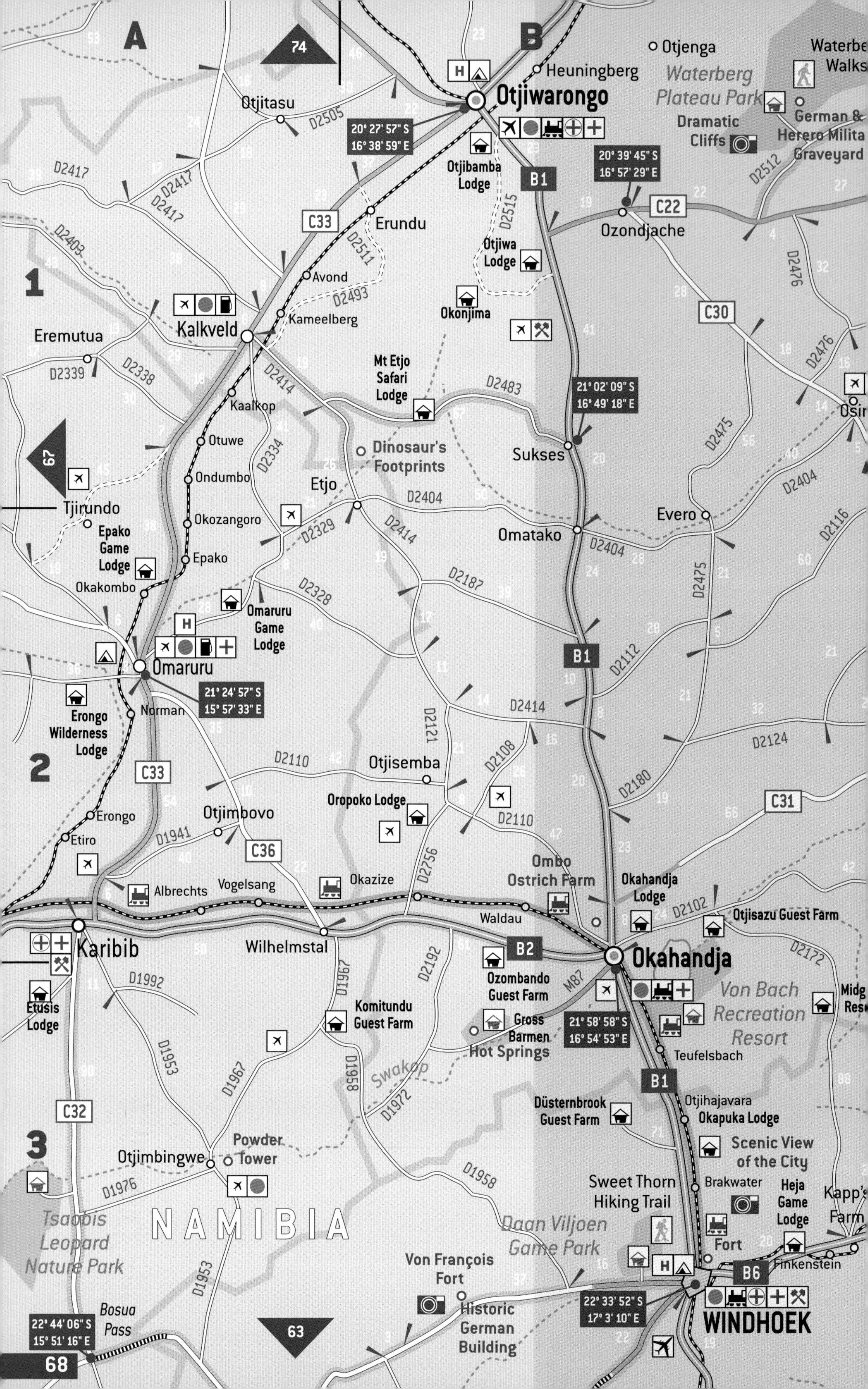

Otjiwarongo
20° 27' 57" S
16° 38' 59" E
Otjiwa Lodge
Otjibamba Lodge
Heuningberg
Otjenga
Waterberg Plateau Park
Dramatic Cliffs
German & Herero Military Graveyard
20° 39' 45" S
16° 57' 29" E
Ozondjache
Erundu
Avond
Kameelberg
Okonjima
Otjitasu
Kalkveld
Eremutua
Kaalkop
Otuwe
Ondumbo
Okozangoro
Epako
Okakombo
Tjirundo
Epako Game Lodge
Mt Etjo Safari Lodge
Dinosaur's Footprints
Etjo
Sukses
21° 02' 09" S
16° 49' 18" E
Evero
Omatako
Omaruru Game Lodge
Omaruru
21° 24' 57" S
15° 57' 33" E
Norman
Erongo Wilderness Lodge
Otjisemba
Oropoko Lodge
Otjimbovo
Erongo
Etiro
Albrechts
Vogelsang
Okazize
Ombo Ostrich Farm
Okahandja Lodge
Otjisazu Guest Farm
Waldau
Karibib
Wilhelmstal
Okahandja
Etusis Lodge
Komitundu Guest Farm
Ozombando Guest Farm
Gross Barmen Hot Springs
21° 58' 58" S
16° 54' 53" E
Von Bach Recreation Resort
Teufelsbach
Swakop
Düsternbrook Guest Farm
Otjihajavara
Okapuka Lodge
Scenic View of the City
Powder Tower
Otjimbingwe
Sweet Thorn Hiking Trail
Brakwater
Heja Game Lodge
NAMIBIA
Tsaobis Leopard Nature Park
Daan Viljoen Game Park
Fort
Finkenstein
Von François Fort
Historic German Building
22° 33' 52" S
17° 3' 10" E
WINDHOEK
Bosua Pass
22° 44' 06" S
15° 51' 16" E
74
67
63

C
D
75
70
64
Otjenga
Waterberg Plateau Park
Waterberg Walks
German & Herero Military Graveyard
Dramatic Cliffs
Otjahevita
Okamatapati
Okakarara
Ozondjache
Hebron
Osire
Evero
Okondjatu
Otjosondu
Summerdown
Hochveld
21° 29' 35" S
17° 51' 16" E
Steinhausen
Okahandja Lodge
Otjisazu Guest Farm
Okahandja
Von Bach Recreation Resort
Midgard Resort
Teufelsbach
Düsternbrook Guest Farm
Otjihajavara
Okapuka Lodge
Scenic View of the City
Brakwater
Heja Game Lodge
Sweet Thorn Hiking Trail
Fort
Finkenstein
Kapp's Farm
WINDHOEK
Auasberge
2479m
Eros
Hosea Kutako
Seeis
Ondekaremba
Nossob
Omitara
Osamba
Diana
Grünental
22° 21' 38" S
18° 02' 06" E
Okasewa
Amhem Cave
B1
B6
C22
C23
C26
C29
C30
C31
C42
M51
M53
M87
M112
D1435
D1468
D1472
D1535
D1643
D1658
D1792
D1800
D1801
D1808
D2102
D2112
D2116
D2120
D2124
D2125
D2135
D2138
D2143
D2146
D2147
D2149
D2166
D2170
D2172
D2177
D2180
D2404
D2446
D2454
D2459
D2460
D2475
D2476
D2512
D3801
D3802
D3803
D3804
D3805
D3826
D1434

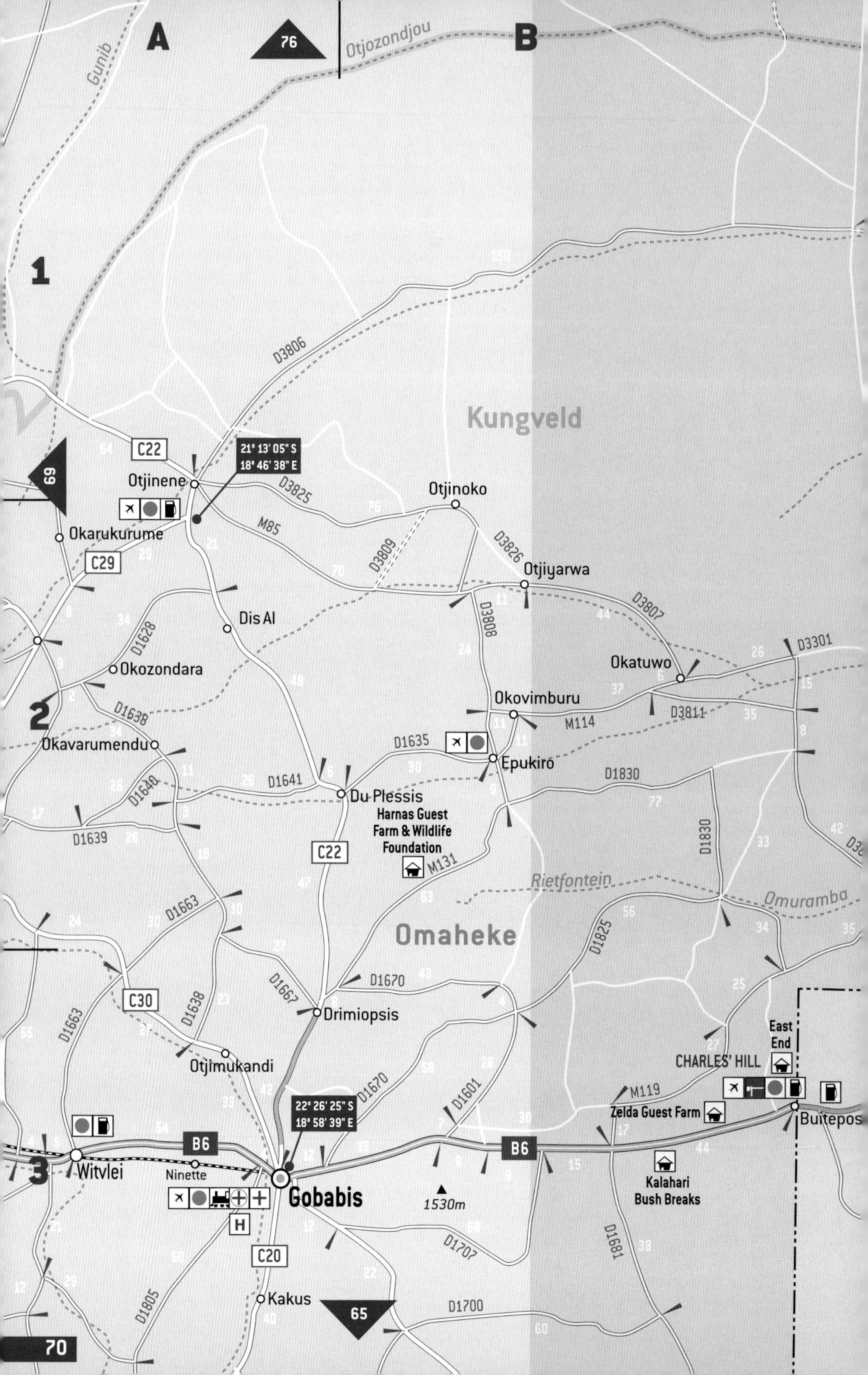
A
B
76
Otjozondjou
Gunib
1
2
3
Kungveld
Omaheke
D3806
C22
69
21° 13' 05" S
18° 46' 38" E
Otjinene
D3825
Otjinoko
Okarukurume
M85
C29
D3809
D3826
Otjiyarwa
D3807
Dis Al
D1628
D3808
Okozondara
Okatuwo
D3301
D1638
Okovimburu
M114
D3811
Okavarumendu
D1635
Epukiro
D1641
D1640
Du Plessis
D1830
Harnas Guest Farm & Wildlife Foundation
D1639
C22
M131
Rietfontein
Omuramba
D1663
D1825
D1670
D1667
C30
D1638
Drimiopsis
D1663
East End
Otjimukandi
CHARLES' HILL
D1670
D1601
M119
22° 26' 25" S
18° 58' 39" E
Zelda Guest Farm
Buitepos
B6
Witvlei
Ninette
B6
Gobabis
1530m
Kalahari Bush Breaks
H
C20
D1707
D1681
D1805
Kakus
65
D1700

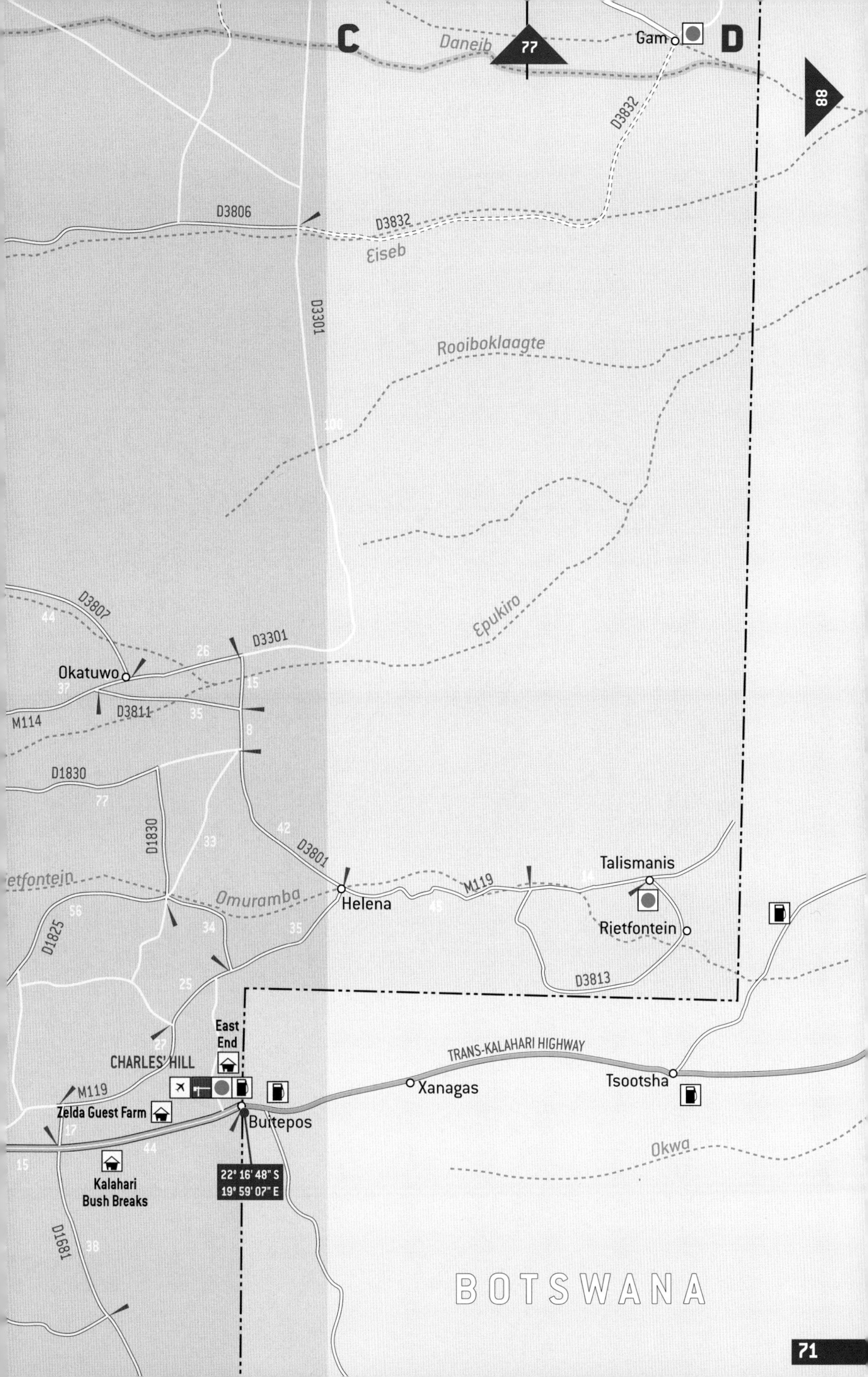

C
D
77
88
Gam
Daneib
D3832
D3806
Eiseb
D3301
Rooiboklaagte
Epukiro
D3807
Okatuwo
M114
D3811
D1830
D3801
Helena
M119
Talismanis
Rietfontein
D3813
Omuramba
D1825
East End
CHARLES' HILL
Zelda Guest Farm
Buitepos
22° 16' 48" S
19° 59' 07" E
Kalahari Bush Breaks
D1681
TRANS-KALAHARI HIGHWAY
Xanagas
Tsootsha
Okwa
BOTSWANA

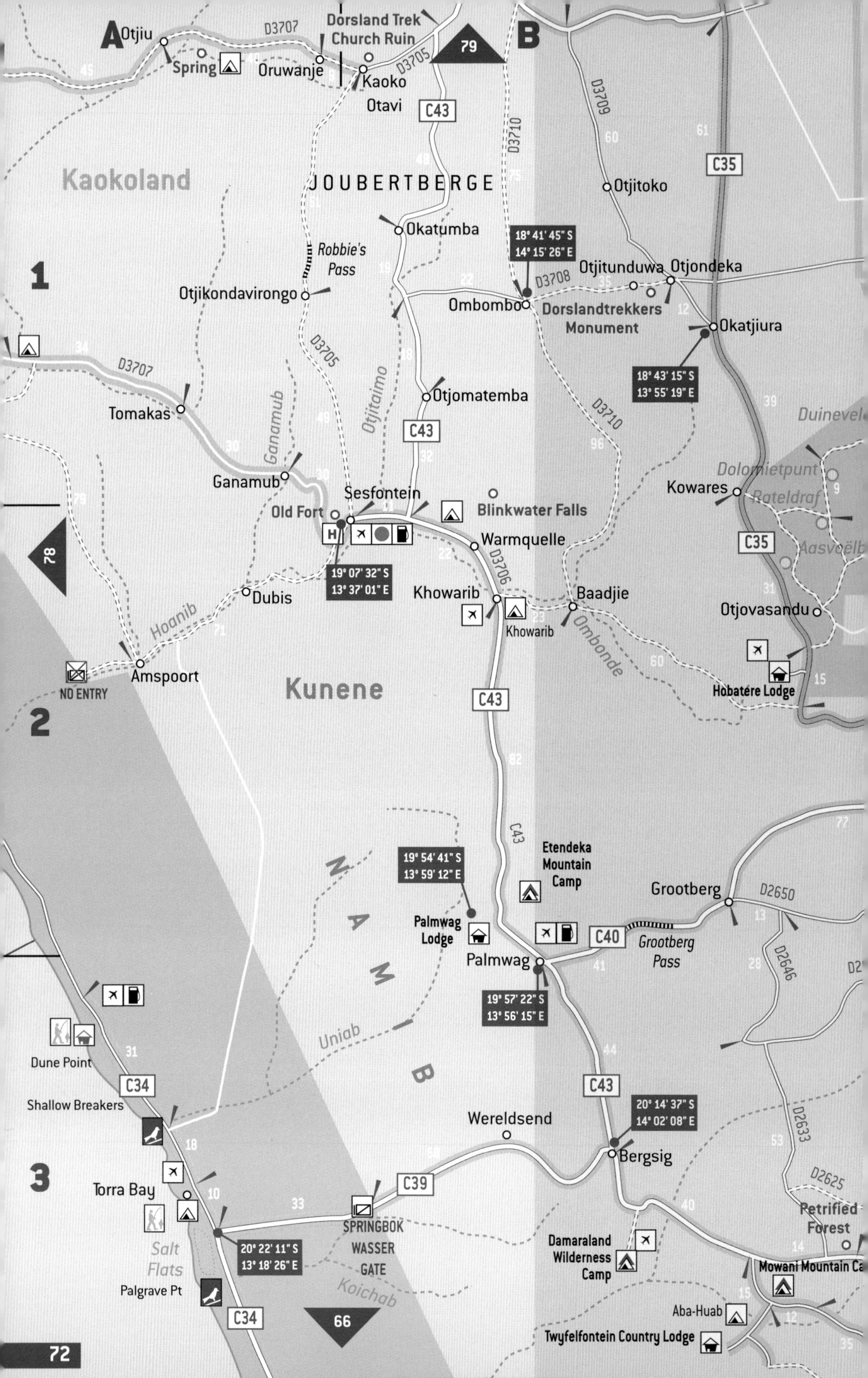
A
B
1
2
3
Otjiu
Spring
Oruwanje
Dorsland Trek Church Ruin
Kaoko Otavi
79
78
66
D3707
D3705
D3709
D3710
D3708
D3706
C43
C35
C40
C39
C34
D2650
D2646
D2633
D2625
Kaokoland
JOUBERTBERGE
Otjitoko
Okatumba
Robbie's Pass
Otjikondavirongo
18° 41' 45" S
14° 15' 26" E
Otjitunduwa
Otjondeka
Ombombo
Dorslandtrekkers Monument
Okatjiura
18° 43' 15" S
13° 55' 19" E
Tomakas
Ganamub
Otjitaimo
Otjomatemba
Duinevel
Dolomietpunt
Rateldraf
Aasvoëlb
Kowares
Sesfontein
Old Fort
Blinkwater Falls
Warmquelle
19° 07' 32" S
13° 37' 01" E
Dubis
Khowarib
Baadjie
Ombonde
Otjovasandu
Hoanib
Amspoort
NO ENTRY
Kunene
Hobatere Lodge
Etendeka Mountain Camp
19° 54' 41" S
13° 59' 12" E
N
A
M
I
B
Grootberg
Grootberg Pass
Palmwag Lodge
Palmwag
19° 57' 22" S
13° 56' 15" E
Uniab
Dune Point
Shallow Breakers
Wereldsend
20° 14' 37" S
14° 02' 08" E
Bergsig
Torra Bay
Salt Flats
Palgrave Pt
20° 22' 11" S
13° 18' 26" E
SPRINGBOK WASSER GATE
Koichab
Damaraland Wilderness Camp
Petrified Forest
Mowani Mountain Ca
Aba-Huab
Twyfelfontein Country Lodge

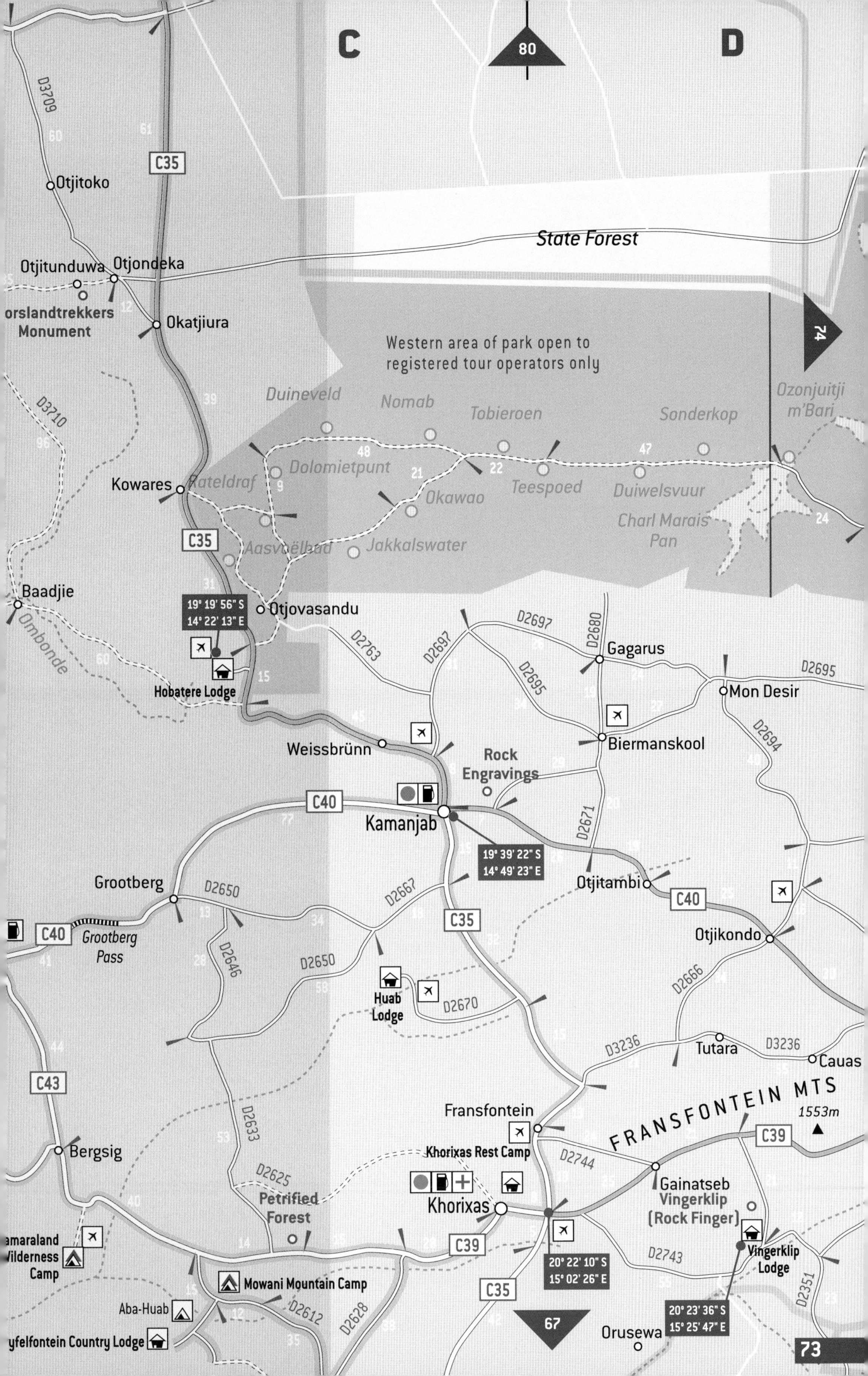

C
D
80
State Forest
74
Western area of park open to registered tour operators only
Otjitoko
Otjitunduwa
Otjondeka
Vorslandtrekkers Monument
Okatjiura
Duineveld
Nomab
Tobieroen
Sonderkop
Ozonjuitji m'Bari
Dolomietpunt
Okawao
Teespoed
Duiwelsvuur
Charl Marais Pan
Kowares
Rateldraf
Aasvoëlbad
Jakkalswater
Baadjie
Ombonde
Otjovasandu
19° 19' 56" S
14° 22' 13" E
Hobatere Lodge
Gagarus
Mon Desir
Biermanskool
Weissbrünn
Rock Engravings
Kamanjab
19° 39' 22" S
14° 49' 23" E
Otjitambi
Grootberg
Grootberg Pass
Otjikondo
Huab Lodge
Tutara
Cauas
FRANSFONTEIN MTS
1553m
Fransfontein
Khorixas Rest Camp
Khorixas
Gainatseb
Vingerklip (Rock Finger)
Vingerklip Lodge
20° 22' 10" S
15° 02' 26" E
20° 23' 36" S
15° 25' 47" E
Bergsig
Petrified Forest
Damaraland Wilderness Camp
Mowani Mountain Camp
Aba-Huab
Twyfelfontein Country Lodge
Orusewa
67
C35
C40
C43
C39
D3709
D3710
D2697
D2680
D2763
D2695
D2694
D2671
D2650
D2667
D2646
D2670
D2666
D3236
D2633
D2625
D2744
D2743
D2612
D2628
D2351

A
B
81
B1
1
2
3
73
68
NEHALE LYA
MPINGANA GATE
Andoni
Toilet
Oshivelo
Natukanaoka
Pan
Cuvelai and
Etosha Pan
Etosha Pan
Groot Okevi
VON
LINDEQUIST
GATE
Etosha
Aoba Lodge
Historic Fort
Klein Okevi
Okerfontein
Namutoni
Toilet
C38
Chudob
Kempinski
Mokuti
Lodge
Springbokfontein
Toilet
Toilet
Okondeka
Rietfontein
Halali
Kalkheuwel
Toilet
19° 10' 44" S
15° 55' 10" E
Okaukuejo
Okaukuejo
Aus
ANDERSSON GATE
Etosha Safari
Lodge & Camp
C38
Toshari
Lodge
19° 35' 34" S
15° 52' 41" E
D2710
D2779
D2782
D2782
D2780
D2761
D2866
D3028
D2865
D3025
D3003
D3031
Guina
Khorab
Memoria
Otavi
C39
D2873
Elefanteberg
Hohental
D2869
D2886
D2869
B1
Komukanti
D2809
Neina
Gamkarab
Cave
Platveld
D2814
D2808
Goreis
C40
Nugubaes
20° 06' 06" S
16° 08' 23" E
Outjo
C39
Vrindskap
D2468
D2775
D2773
Okaputa
D2804
Otjikango
D2433
Waterberg
Plateau Park
Waterberg
Wilderness
Trail
C38
Hartseer
M63
Ugab
D2752
20° 27' 57" S
16° 38' 59" E
D2430
Okave
Otjenga
Heuningberg
Waterberg Walks
Otjitasu
D2427
D2505
Otjiwarongo
Otjibamba Lodge
Dramatic
Cliffs
D2512
D2477

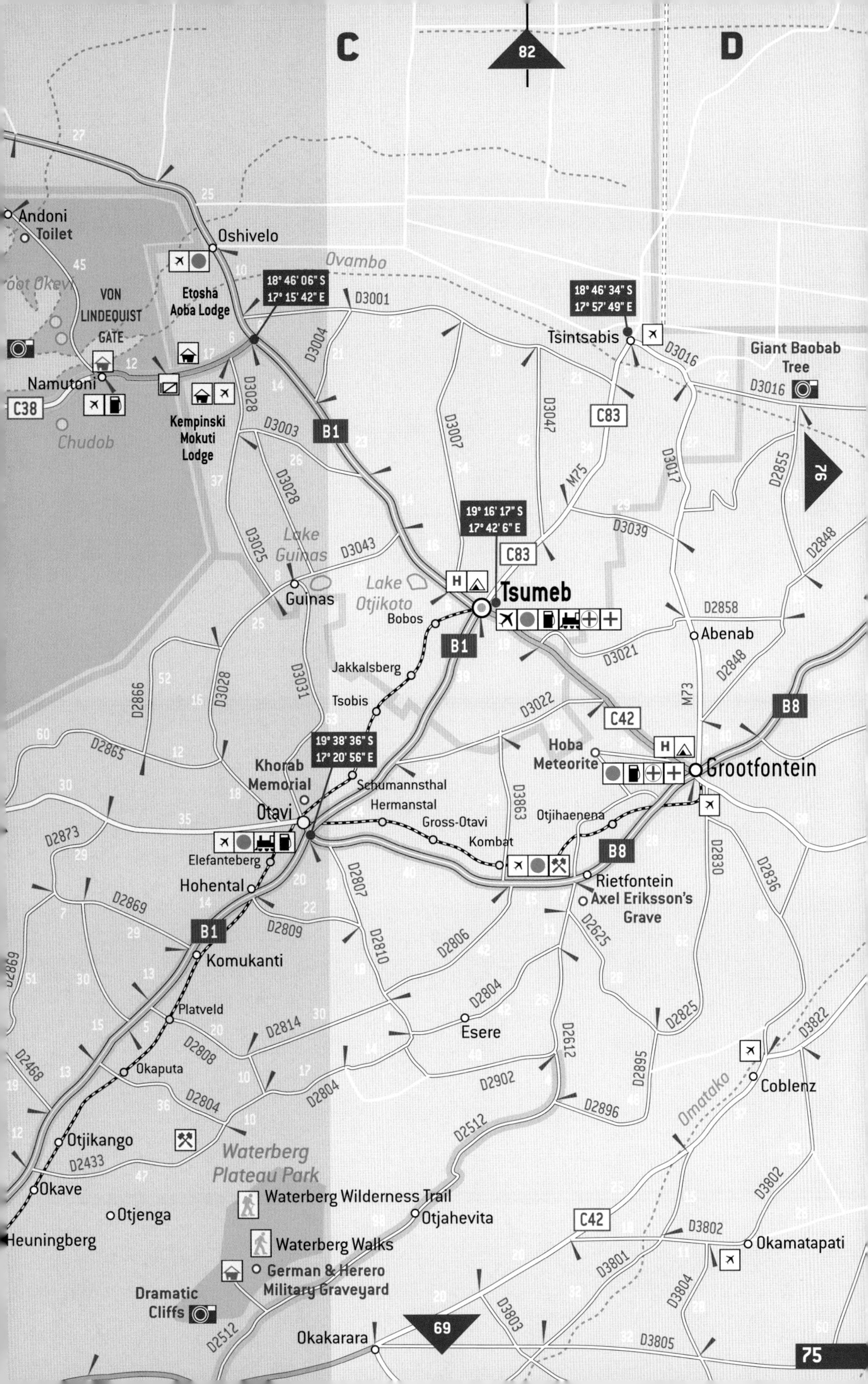

C
D
82
Andoni
Toilet
Oshivelo
Ovambo
VON
LINDEQUIST
GATE
Etosha
Aoba Lodge
18° 46' 06" S
17° 15' 42" E
D3001
18° 46' 34" S
17° 57' 49" E
Tsintsabis
D3016
Giant Baobab
Tree
Namutoni
C38
Kempinski
Mokuti
Lodge
Chudob
D3004
D3028
D3003
B1
D3007
D3047
C83
M75
D3017
D2855
76
19° 16' 17" S
17° 42' 6" E
D3039
Lake
Guinas
D3043
D3025
C83
D2848
Guinas
Lake
Otjikoto
Tsumeb
Bobos
D2858
Abenab
D3021
D2848
Jakkalsberg
Tsobis
D3031
D3028
D2866
D3022
M73
C42
B8
D2865
19° 38' 36" S
17° 20' 56" E
Khorab
Memorial
Hoba
Meteorite
Grootfontein
Schumannsthal
Hermanstal
Gross-Otavi
D3863
Otjihaenena
Otavi
D2873
Kombat
Elefanteberg
B8
D2830
D2836
Hohental
D2807
Rietfontein
Axel Eriksson's
Grave
D2869
D2809
D2810
D2806
D2625
B1
Komukanti
D2869
D2804
D2825
Platveld
D2814
Esere
D2612
D3822
D2808
D2895
D2468
Okaputa
D2902
Omatako
Coblenz
D2804
D2804
D2896
Otjikango
D2512
D2433
Waterberg
Plateau Park
D3802
Okave
Waterberg Wilderness Trail
Otjenga
Otjahevita
C42
Heuningberg
Waterberg Walks
D3802
Okamatapati
German & Herero
Military Graveyard
D3801
Dramatic
Cliffs
D3804
D3803
69
D2512
Okakarara
D3805

A
83
B
B8
Ncaute
1
Mangetti
75
Mururani
D3016
D2908
D3016
D2848
Maanlig
D2898
Karakuwisa
C44
Maroelaboom
Kano Vlei
19° 14' 54" S
18° 29' 45" E
D2845
D2868
D2893
Nhoma
Omatako
Luhebu
D3312
D2844
2
D3306
D2874
C44
Aasvoëln
D2874
Otjituuo
D2803
C42
D3800
D2803
D3300
D3301
D3306
Tweeputte
Otjozondjupa
D3805
3
Otjozondjou
Gunib
NAMIBIA
70

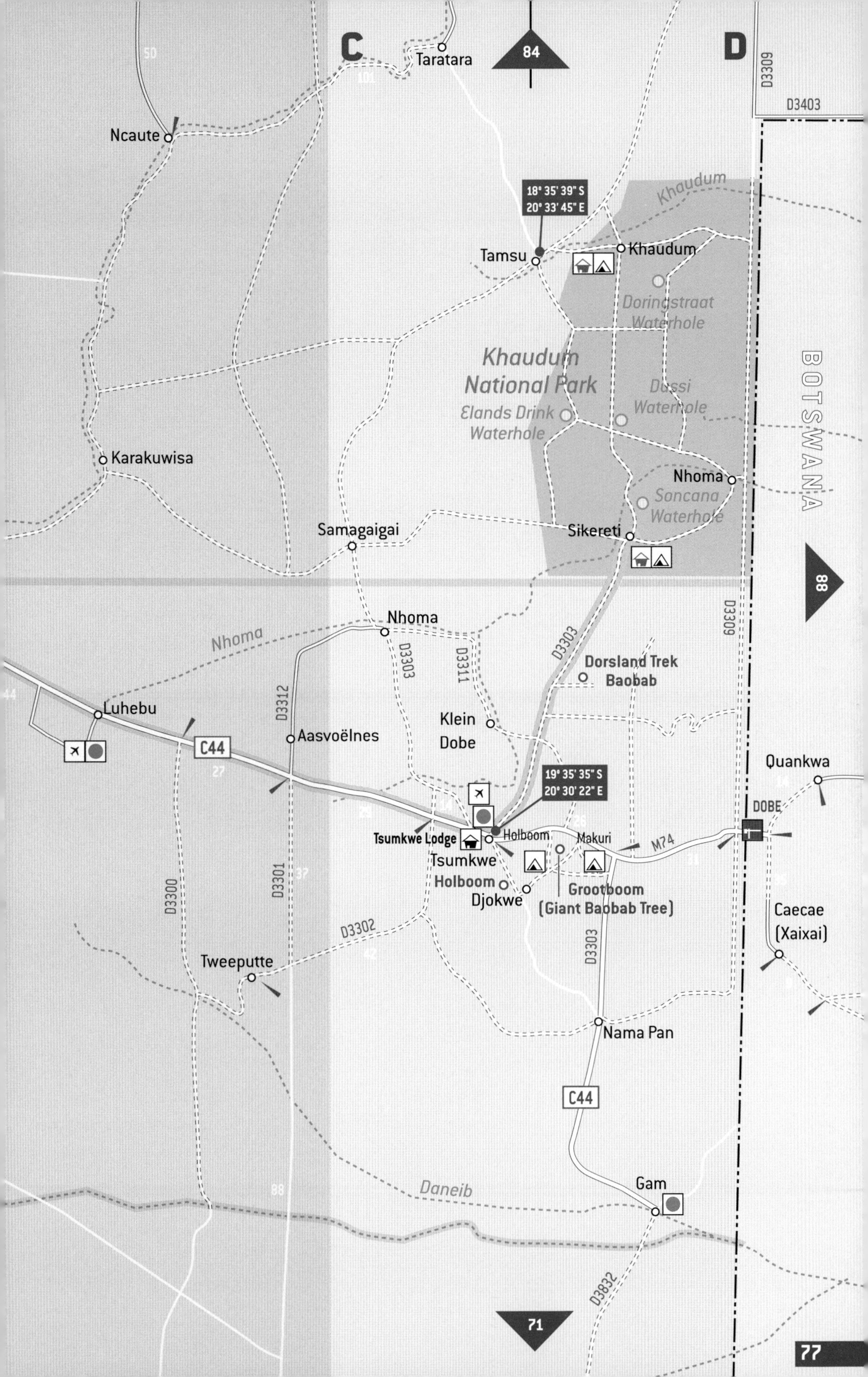

C
D
84
Taratara
50
101
Ncaute
D3309
D3403
Khaudum
18° 35' 39" S
20° 33' 45" E
Tamsu
Khaudum
Doringstraat Waterhole
Khaudum National Park
Dussi Waterhole
Elands Drink Waterhole
BOTSWANA
Karakuwisa
Nhoma
Soncana Waterhole
Samagaigai
Sikereti
88
D3309
Nhoma
Nhoma
D3303
D3311
D3303
Dorsland Trek Baobab
D3312
Luhebu
Klein Dobe
Aasvoëlnes
C44
27
Quankwa
19° 35' 35" S
20° 30' 22" E
DOBE
Tsumkwe Lodge
Holboom
Makuri
M74
Tsumkwe
Holboom
Djokwe
Grootboom (Giant Baobab Tree)
D3300
D3301
Caecae (Xaixai)
D3302
D3303
Tweeputte
Nama Pan
C44
Gam
Daneib
D3832
71

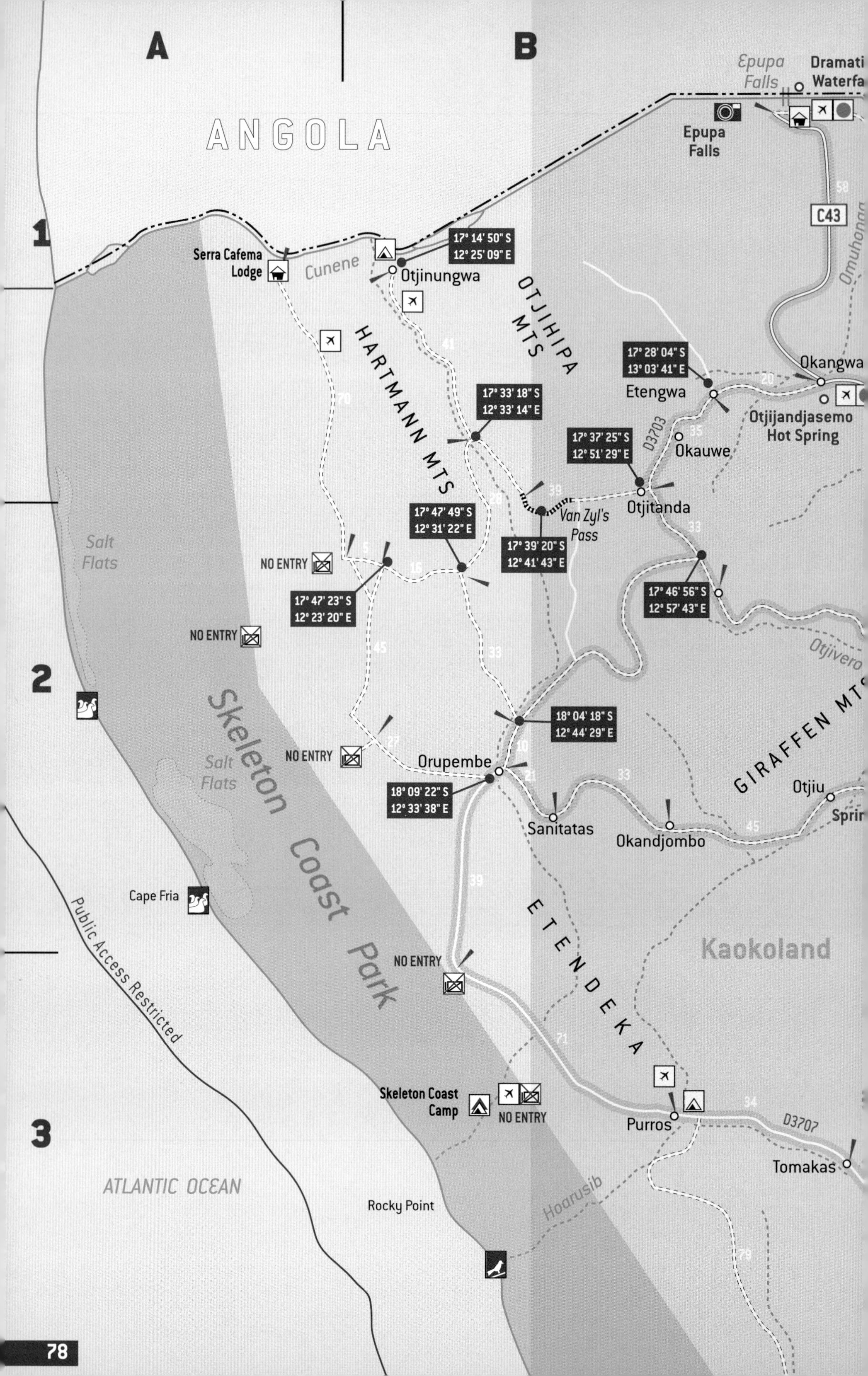

A
B
ANGOLA
Epupa Falls
Dramati Waterfa
Epupa Falls
58
C43
Omuhonga
1
Serra Cafema Lodge
Cunene
17° 14' 50" S
12° 25' 09" E
Otjinungwa
OTJIHIPA MTS
HARTMANN MTS
41
70
17° 28' 04" S
13° 03' 41" E
Etengwa
20
Okangwa
Otjijandjasemo Hot Spring
17° 33' 18" S
12° 33' 14" E
D3703
35
Okauwe
17° 37' 25" S
12° 51' 29" E
Otjitanda
39
Van Zyl's Pass
28
17° 47' 49" S
12° 31' 22" E
17° 39' 20" S
12° 41' 43" E
33
Salt Flats
NO ENTRY
5
15
17° 47' 23" S
12° 23' 20" E
17° 46' 56" S
12° 57' 43" E
NO ENTRY
45
33
Otjivero
2
GIRAFFEN MTS
Skeleton Coast Park
18° 04' 18" S
12° 44' 29" E
NO ENTRY
27
10
Salt Flats
Orupembe
21
33
18° 09' 22" S
12° 33' 38" E
Otjiu
Sanitatas
Okandjombo
45
Sprir
39
Cape Fria
ETENDEKA
Public Access Restricted
Kaokoland
NO ENTRY
71
Skeleton Coast Camp
NO ENTRY
Purros
34
D3707
3
Tomakas
ATLANTIC OCEAN
Rocky Point
Hoarusib
79

C
D
ANGOLA
Epupa Falls
Dramatic Waterfall
Epupa Falls
17° 00' 09" S 13° 14' 39" E
C43
Enyandi
Omuhonga
17° 13' 40" S 13° 14' 11" E
ZEBRA MTS
D3700
17° 20' 28" S 13° 50' 56" E
View of Waterfall
Ruacana Falls
Swartbooisdrift
17° 26' 01" S 13° 16' 20" E
Okangwati
Kunene River Lodge
Ruacana
Etengwa
Otjijandjasemo Hot Spring
Epembe
Ondoto
D3702
Ehomba
D3703
Okauwe
Otjiveze
17° 37' 23" S 13° 28' 34" E
State Forest
Otjitanda
Van Zyl's Pass
STEILRAND MTS
D3700
D3720
C35
17° 51' 45" S 13° 01' 26" E
Etanga
Otjivero
D3703
18° 03' 29" S 13° 15' 31" E
80
Opuwo
GIRAFFEN MTS
Hoarusib
Dorsland Trek Church Ruin
C41
Otjiu
D3707
18° 08' 39" S 14° 17' 26" E
Okandjombo
Sanitatas
Spring
Oruwanje
Kaoko
D3705
Otavi
C43
D3709
D3710
Kaokoland
JOUBERTBERGE
C35
Otjitoko
TENDEKA
Okatumba
18° 41' 45" S 14° 15' 26" E
Robbie's Pass
Otjitunduwa
Otjondeka
D3708
Otjikondavirongo
Ombombo
Dorslandtrekkers Monument
Okatjiura
D3705
18° 43' 15" S 13° 55' 19" E
Purros
D3707
Otjitaimo
Otjomatemba
D3710
Tomakas
C43
Hoarusib
Ganamub
19° 07' 32" S 13° 37' 01" E
Ganamub
Sesfontein
Kowares
Old Fort
Blinkwater Falls
Fort Sesfontein
Warmquelle
72
D3706
Khowarib
Khowarib

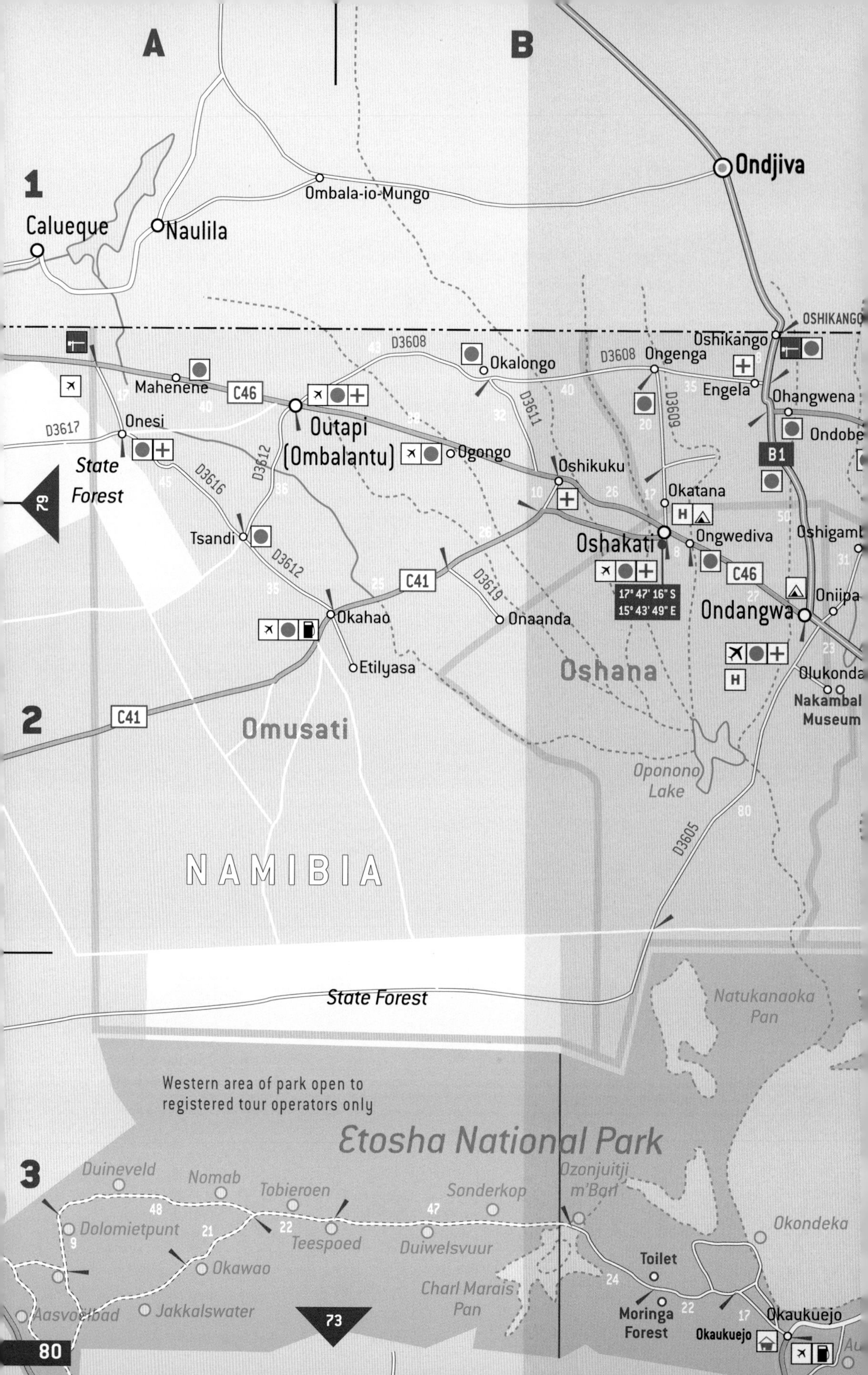

A
B
1
2
3
Ondjiva
Ombala-io-Mungo
Calueque
Naulila
OSHIKANGO
Oshikango
D3608
Okalongo
Ongenga
Engela
Ohangwena
Ondobe
Mahenene
C46
Outapi
(Ombalantu)
Onesi
D3617
State
Forest
79
D3616
D3612
Ogongo
D3611
D3609
Oshikuku
Okatana
B1
Tsandi
Oshakati
Ongwediva
Oshigambo
17° 47' 16" S
15° 43' 49" E
C41
D3619
Okahao
Onaanda
Ondangwa
Oniipa
Etilyasa
Oshana
Olukonda
Nakambale
Museum
Omusati
Oponono
Lake
D3605
NAMIBIA
State Forest
Natukanaoka
Pan
Western area of park open to
registered tour operators only
Etosha National Park
Duineveld
Nomab
Tobieroen
Sonderkop
Ozonjuitji
m'Bari
Dolomietpunt
Teespoed
Duiwelsvuur
Okondeka
Okawao
Toilet
Charl Marais
Pan
Aasvoëlbad
Jakkalswater
73
Moringa
Forest
Okaukuejo

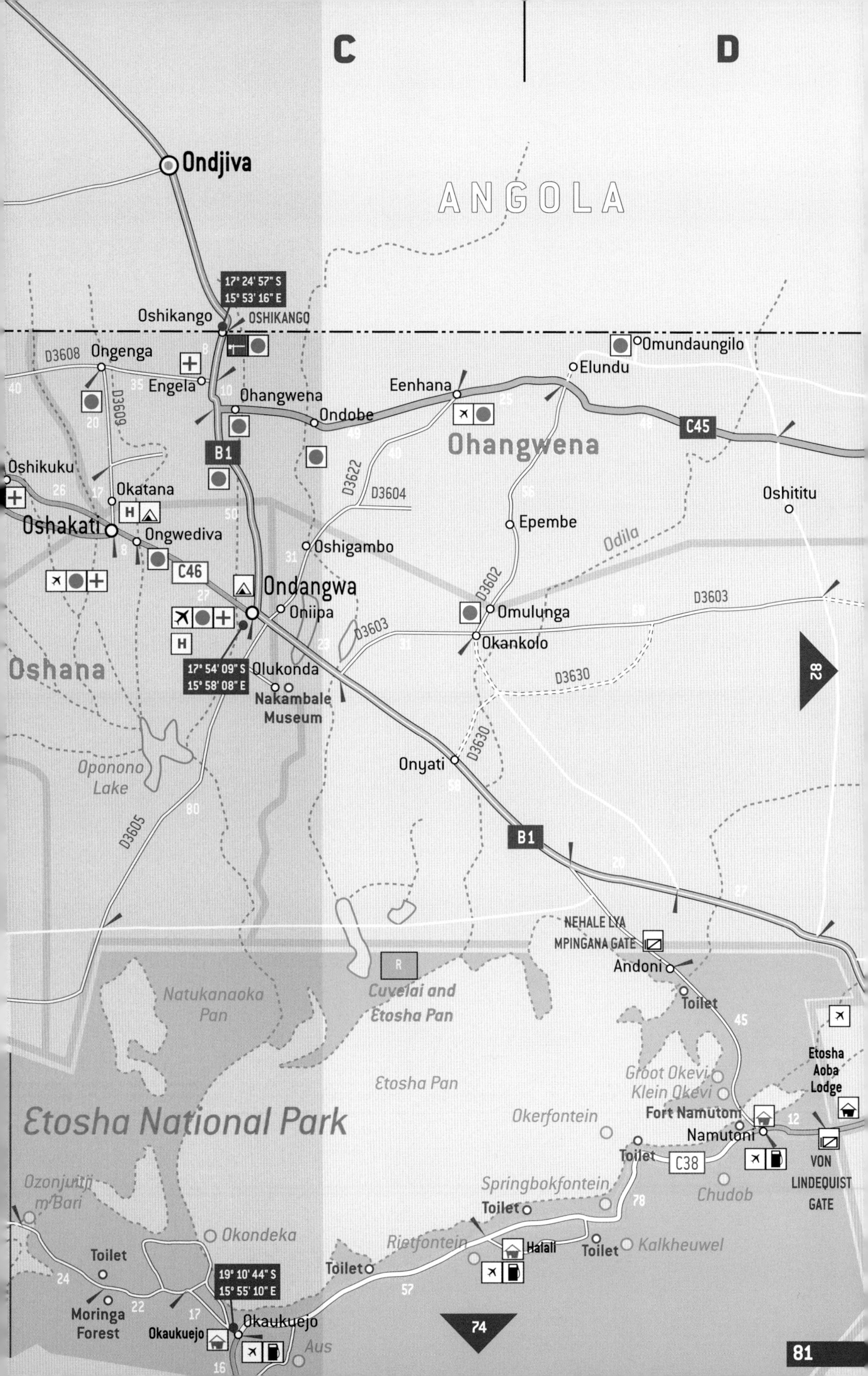
C
D
Ondjiva
ANGOLA
17° 24' 57" S
15° 53' 16" E
Oshikango
OSHIKANGO
D3608
Ongenga
Engela
Ohangwena
Ondobe
Eenhana
Elundu
Omundaungilo
C45
Ohangwena
B1
D3609
Oshikuku
Okatana
Oshakati
Ongwediva
C46
D3622
D3604
Oshigambo
Epembe
Odila
Oshititu
Ondangwa
Oniipa
D3602
Omulunga
D3603
Okankolo
D3630
Oshana
17° 54' 09" S
15° 58' 08" E
Olukonda
Nakambale Museum
Onyati
Oponono Lake
D3605
NEHALE LYA MPINGANA GATE
Andoni
Toilet
Natukanaoka Pan
Cuvelai and Etosha Pan
Etosha Pan
Groot Okevi
Klein Okevi
Fort Namutoni
Namutoni
Etosha Aoba Lodge
Okerfontein
Etosha National Park
Toilet
C38
VON LINDEQUIST GATE
Ozonjuitji m'Bari
Springbokfontein
Chudob
Toilet
Okondeka
Rietfontein
Halali
Toilet
Kalkheuwel
Toilet
19° 10' 44" S
15° 55' 10" E
Toilet
Moringa Forest
Okaukuejo
Okaukuejo
Aus
28
74

A
B
ANGOLA
1
2
3
State Forest
Okongo
Ekoko
B10
C45
D3404
D3405
D3407
Kavango
Cuangar
Nkurenkuru
Mpungu
D3406
Nepara
Tondoro
81
D3600
Oshikoto
Tsitsib
Khaudum
D3444
NAMIBIA
D3610
D3445
Oshivelo
Ovambo
18° 46' 06" S
17° 15' 42" E
D3001
18° 46' 34" S
17° 57' 49" E
Tsintsabis
Mangetti
Giant Baobab Tree
D3016
D3004
D3028
D3003
B1
D3007
D3047
C83
D3017
D2855
D2908
D2848
19° 16' 17" S
17° 42' 6" E
D3039
Lake Guinas
D3043
D3025
Guinas
75
19° 14' 54" S
18° 29' 45" E
Roy's Rest Camp
B8

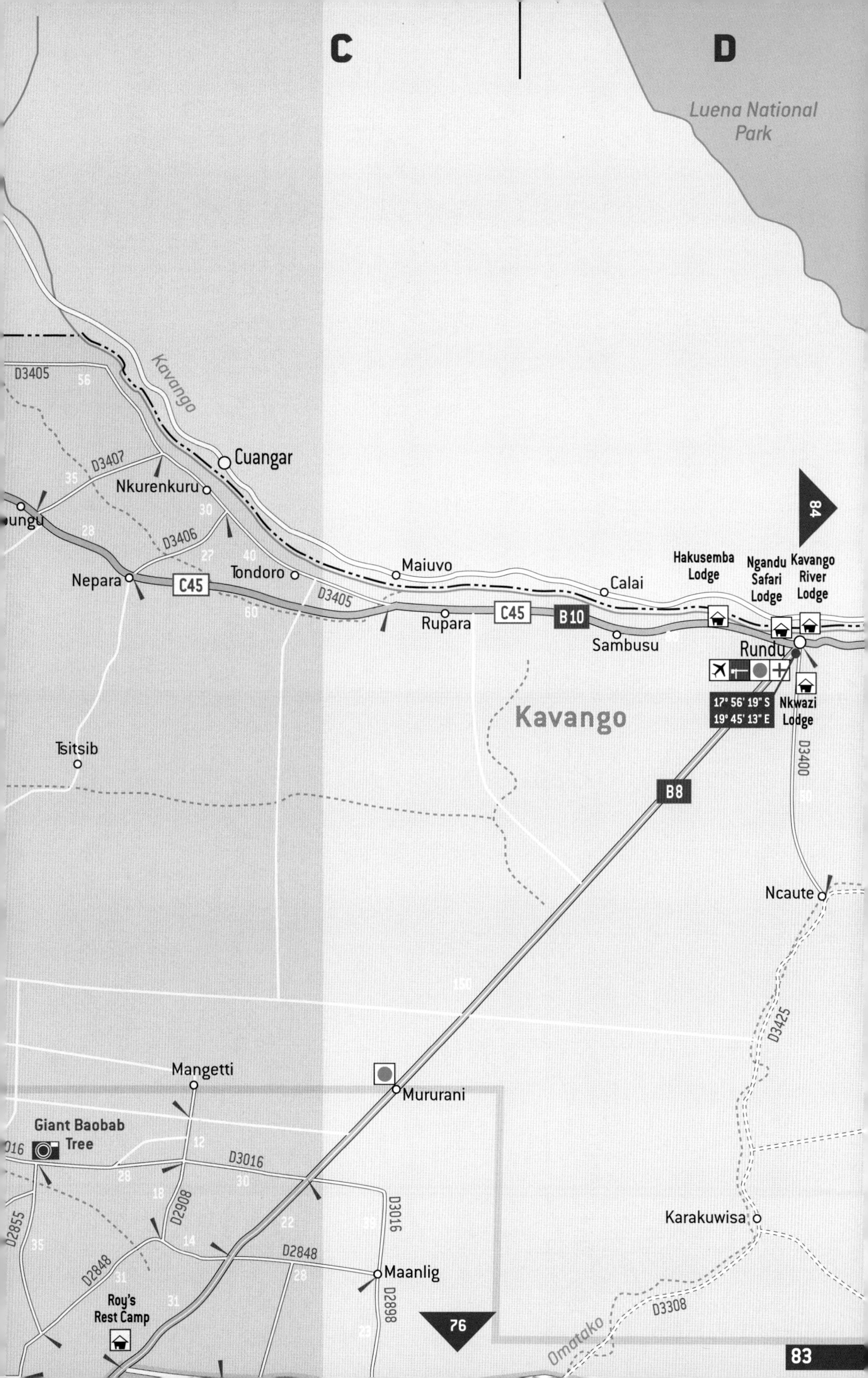
C
D
Luena National Park
Kavango
D3405
56
D3407
35
Cuangar
Nkurenkuru
30
28
D3406
27
40
Nepara
C45
Tondoro
D3405
60
Maiuvo
Calai
Rupara
C45
B10
Sambusu
Hakusemba Lodge
Ngandu Safari Lodge
Kavango River Lodge
84
Rundu
17° 56' 19" S
19° 45' 13" E
Nkwazi Lodge
Kavango
D3400
50
Tsitsib
B8
Ncaute
150
D3425
Mangetti
Mururani
Giant Baobab Tree
D3016
12
28
30
18
D2908
D3016
D2855
35
22
39
14
D2848
D2848
31
28
Maanlig
Roy's Rest Camp
31
D2898
76
Karakuwisa
D3308
Omatako

A
B
1
2
3
Cuito
Mucusso National Park
Utokota
Mashari
Dirico
Nyangana
B8
Mucusso
Mukwe
Divundu
Mahango Core Area
D3400
Taratara
83
D3309
D3403
Kavango
18° 35' 39" S
20° 33' 45" E
Khaudum
Nxamasere
Tamsu
Khaudum
Doringstraat Waterhole
Tsodilo Hills
R
Khaudum National Park
Elands Drink Waterhole
Dussi Waterhole
Nhoma
Soncana Waterhole
Sikereti
Samagaigai
Nhoma
Nhoma
D3303
D3311
D3303
Dorsland Trek Baobab
D3312
Aasvoëlnes
Klein Dobe
D3315
19° 35' 35" S
20° 30' 22" E
Quankwa
DOBE
Tsumkwe Lodge
Holboom
Makuri
M74
D3301
Tsumkwe
Otjozondjupa
Holboom
Djokwe
Grootboom (Giant Baobab Tree)
77

C D

ANGOLA

Mucusso National Park

Zambezi Region

Bwabwata National Park

B8 200

Mucusso

18° 5' 58" S
21° 32' 48" E

B8 81

Mukwe

Divundu

Popa Falls

Suclabo Lodge

Ndhovu Safari Lodge

Omega

Mahango Core Area

D3403

MOHEMBO
06:00 - 18:00

18° 15' 28" S
21° 45' 32" E

98

Drotsky's Cabins

Shakawe

Shakawe Fishing Lodge

Nxamasere

Sengoshe

Okavango

Tsodilo Hills

R

Rock Paintings

Nxamasere

Dibebe

Sepupa

Mawana

Dungu

Swamp Stop

Seronga

Cada

Gqoro

Eretse

18° 44' 35" S
22° 10' 16" E

Guma Lagoon

Etsha

Xaudum

Makwena Lodge

Jedibe

Etsha 6

Jao

BOTSWANA

Qhaakwe

Thaoge

Abu's

Okavango Delta

Gumare

Quankwa

Xudum

SANDVELDT TONGUE

Nokaneng

19° 40' 6" S
22° 11' 40" E

88

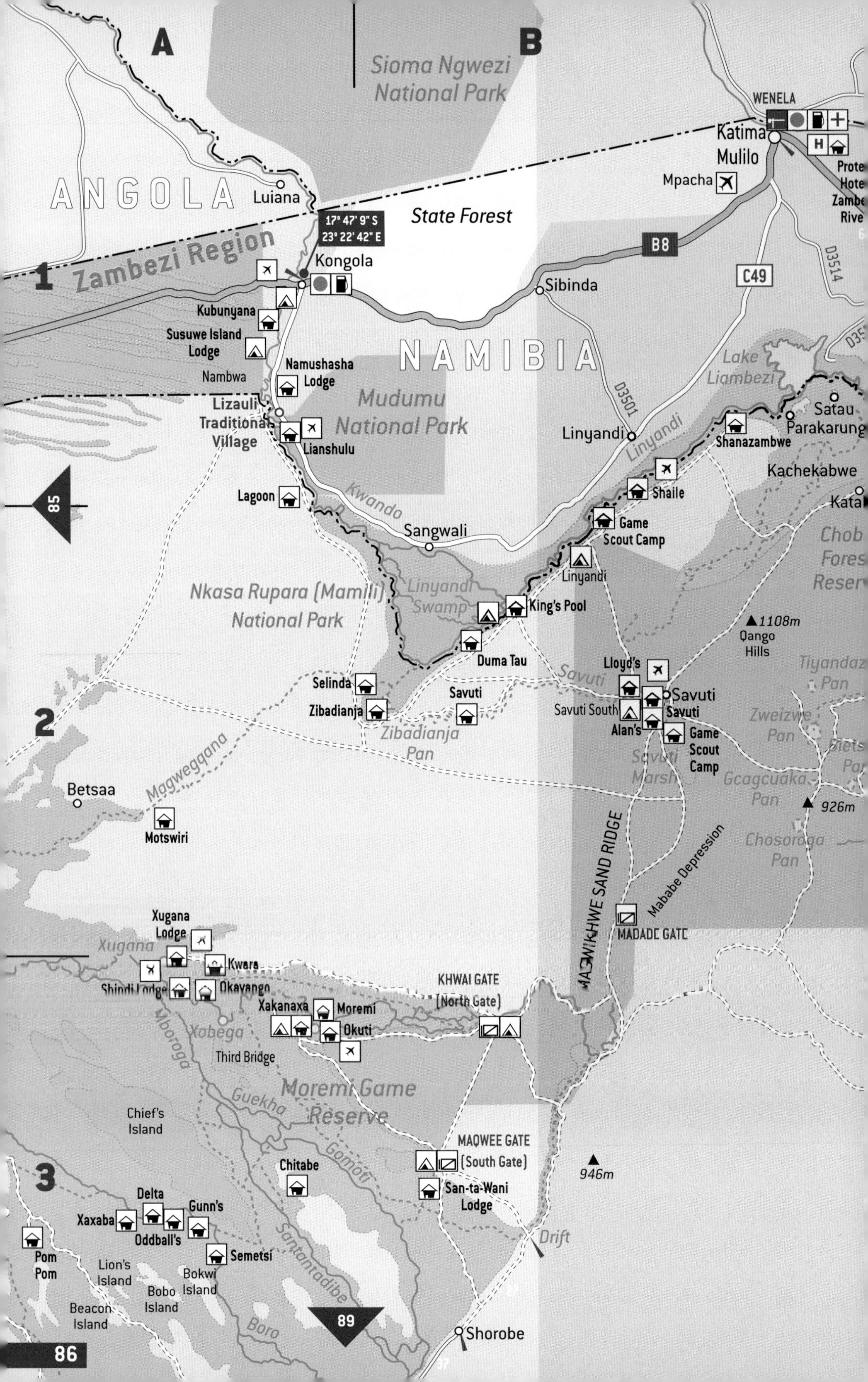

A
B
Sioma Ngwezi National Park
WENELA
Katima Mulilo
Mpacha
ANGOLA
Luiana
17° 47' 9" S
23° 22' 42" E
State Forest
B8
Zambezi Region
Kongola
Sibinda
C49
D3514
Kubunyana
Susuwe Island Lodge
Namushasha Lodge
NAMIBIA
Lake Liambezi
Nambwa
Mudumu National Park
Lizauli Traditional Village
Lianshulu
D3501
Linyandi
Satau
Parakarung
Shanazambwe
Kachekabwe
85
Lagoon
Kwando
Shaile
Game Scout Camp
Sangwali
Linyandi
Linyandi Swamp
Nkasa Rupara (Mamili) National Park
King's Pool
Duma Tau
1108m
Qango Hills
Lloyd's
Savuti
Selinda
Zibadianja
Savuti South
Alan's
Game Scout Camp
Zibadianja Pan
Zweizwe Pan
Magwegqana
Savuti Marsh
Gcagcuaka Pan
Betsaa
Motswiri
926m
Chosoroga Pan
MAGWIKHWE SAND RIDGE
Mababe Depression
MABABE GATE
Xugana Lodge
Xugana
Kwara
Shindi Lodge
Okavango
KHWAI GATE (North Gate)
Xakanaxa
Moremi
Okuti
Xobega
Mboroga
Third Bridge
Moremi Game Reserve
Guekha
Chief's Island
Gomoti
MAQWEE GATE (South Gate)
Chitabe
946m
San-ta-Wani Lodge
Delta
Gunn's
Xaxaba
Oddball's
Drift
Semetsi
Pom Pom
Lion's Island
Bokwi Island
Bobo Island
Santantadibe
Beacon Island
89
Boro
Shorobe
1
2
3

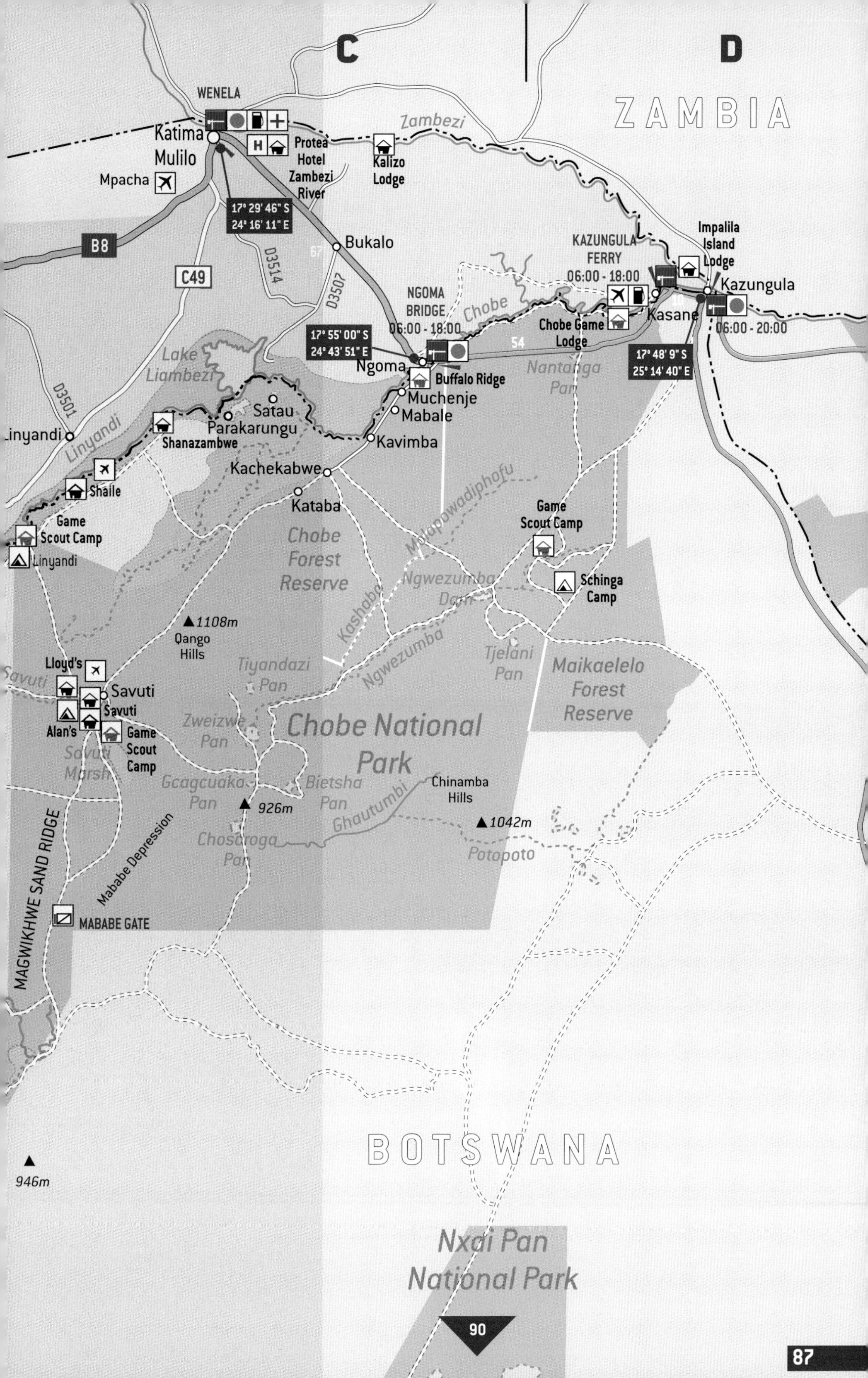

C
D
ZAMBIA
WENELA
Katima Mulilo
Mpacha
17° 29' 46" S
24° 16' 11" E
Protea Hotel Zambezi River
Kalizo Lodge
Zambezi
B8
C49
D3514
D3507
67
Bukalo
KAZUNGULA FERRY
06:00 - 18:00
Impalila Island Lodge
Kazungula
Kasane
10
06:00 - 20:00
17° 48' 9" S
25° 14' 40" E
NGOMA BRIDGE
06:00 - 18:00
Chobe
Chobe Game Lodge
54
17° 55' 00" S
24° 43' 51" E
Ngoma
Buffalo Ridge
Nantanga Pan
Lake Liambezi
D3501
Linyandi
Satau
Parakarungu
Muchenje
Mabale
Kavimba
Shanazambwe
Kachekabwe
Kataba
Shaile
Game Scout Camp
Linyandi
Chobe Forest Reserve
Molapowadiphofu
Game Scout Camp
Schinga Camp
Ngwezumba Dam
Kashaba
1108m
Qango Hills
Lloyd's
Savuti
Savuti
Savuti
Alan's
Game Scout Camp
Tiyandazi Pan
Ngwezumba
Tjelani Pan
Maikaelelo Forest Reserve
Zweizwe Pan
Chobe National Park
Savuti Marsh
Gcagcuaka Pan
926m
Bietsha Pan
Ghautumbi
Chinamba Hills
1042m
Chosaroga Pan
Potopoto
Mababe Depression
MAGWIKHWE SAND RIDGE
MABABE GATE
946m
BOTSWANA
Nxai Pan National Park
90

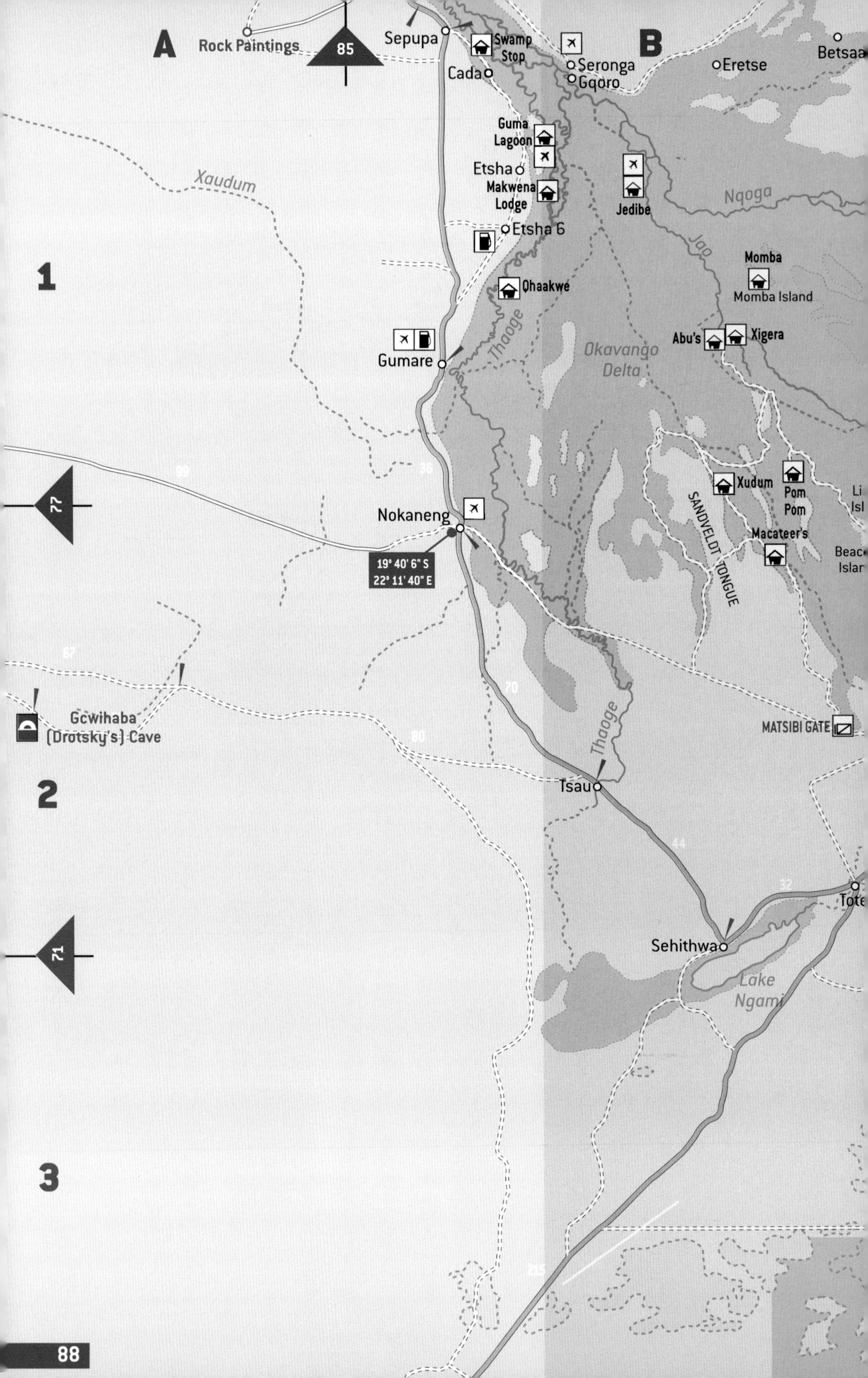
A
B
1
2
3
85
77
71
Rock Paintings
Sepupa
Swamp Stop
Cada
Seronga
Gqoro
Eretse
Betsaa
Guma Lagoon
Etsha
Makwena Lodge
Etsha 6
Jedibe
Xaudum
Ngoga
Jao
Momba
Momba Island
Qhaakwe
Thaoge
Okavango Delta
Gumare
Abu's
Xigera
Xudum
Pom Pom
SANDVELDT TONGUE
Macateer's
Nokaneng
19° 40' 6" S
22° 11' 40" E
Gcwihaba (Drotsky's) Cave
MATSIBI GATE
Tsau
Sehithwa
Lake Ngami
Tote
99
36
67
70
80
44
32
215

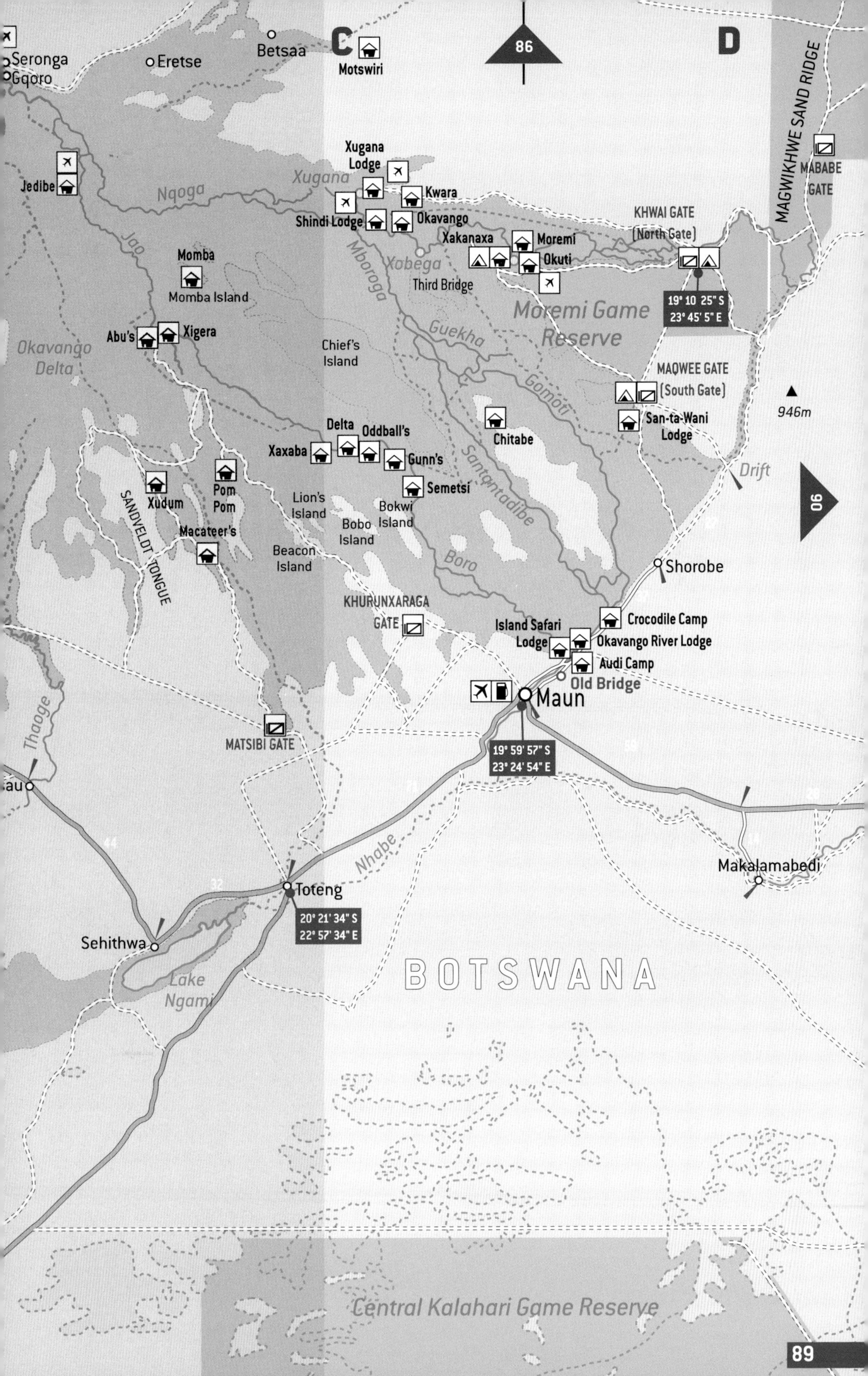
C
D
86
90
Seronga
Gqoro
Eretse
Betsaa
Motswiri
MAGWIKHWE SAND RIDGE
MABABE GATE
Jedibe
Xugana Lodge
Xugana
Ngoga
Kwara
Shindi Lodge
Okavango
Xakanaxa
Moremi
Okuti
KHWAI GATE (North Gate)
Jao
Mboroga
Xobega
Third Bridge
Momba
Momba Island
19° 10' 25" S
23° 45' 5" E
Moremi Game Reserve
Abu's
Xigera
Guekha
Okavango Delta
Chief's Island
Gomoti
MAQWEE GATE (South Gate)
946m
San-ta-Wani Lodge
Delta
Oddball's
Chitabe
Xaxaba
Gunn's
Drift
Xudum
Pom Pom
Semetsi
Santantadibe
SANDVELDT TONGUE
Lion's Island
Bokwi Island
Bobo Island
Macateer's
Beacon Island
Boro
Shorobe
KHURUNXARAGA GATE
Crocodile Camp
Island Safari Lodge
Okavango River Lodge
Audi Camp
Old Bridge
Maun
Thaoge
MATSIBI GATE
19° 59' 57" S
23° 24' 54" E
Nhabe
Makalamabedi
Toteng
20° 21' 34" S
22° 57' 34" E
Sehithwa
Lake Ngami
BOTSWANA
Central Kalahari Game Reserve

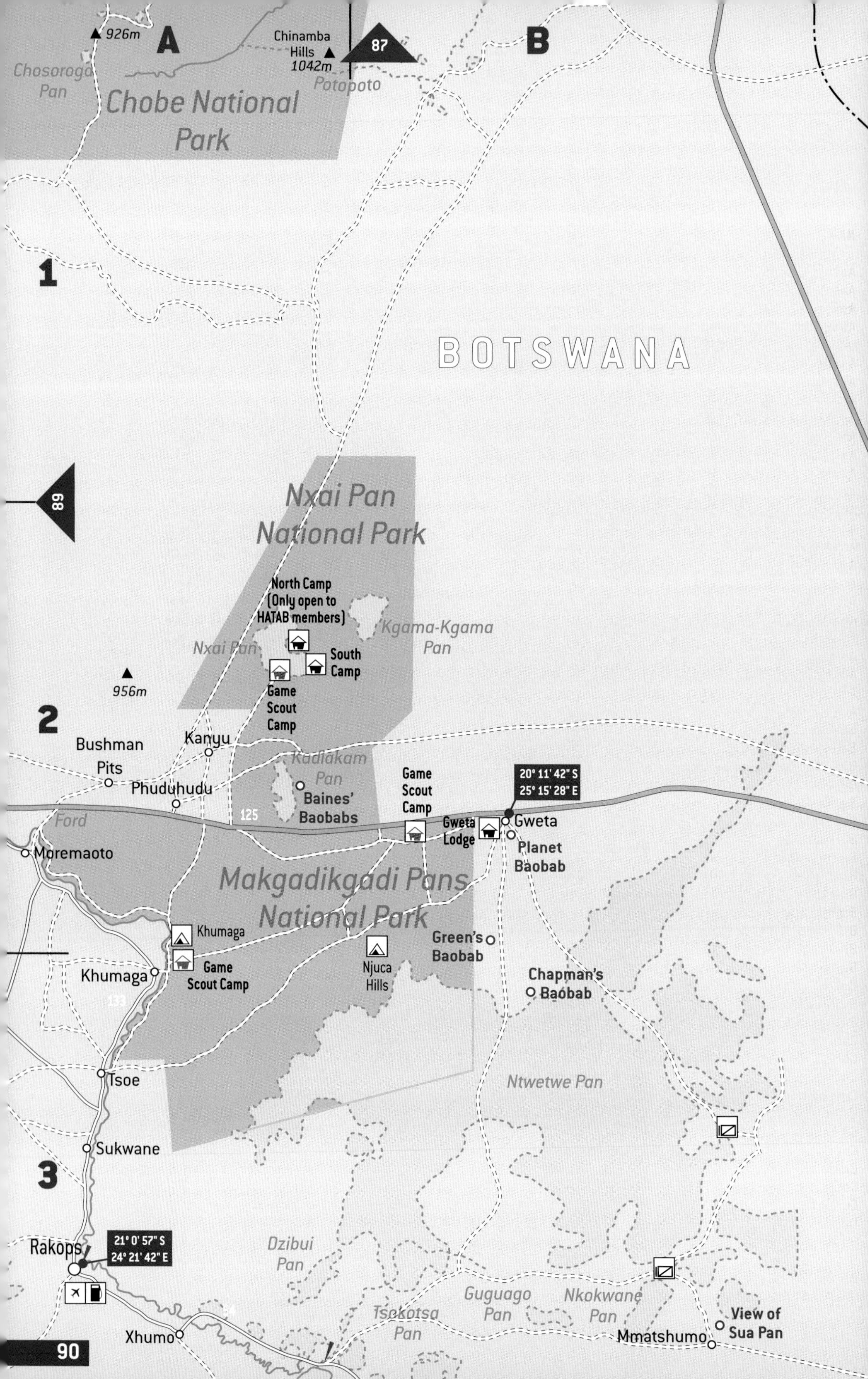
926m
A
Chinamba
Hills
1042m
87
B
Chosorogo
Pan
Potopoto
Chobe National
Park
1
BOTSWANA
89
Nxai Pan
National Park
North Camp
(Only open to
HATAB members)
Kgama-Kgama
Pan
Nxai Pan
South
Camp
956m
Game
Scout
Camp
2
Kanyu
Bushman
Pits
Kudiakam
Pan
Game
Scout
Camp
20° 11' 42" S
25° 15' 28" E
Phuduhudu
Baines'
Baobabs
125
Ford
Gweta
Lodge
Gweta
Planet
Baobab
Moremaoto
Makgadikgadi Pans
National Park
Khumaga
Game
Scout Camp
Khumaga
Njuca
Hills
Green's
Baobab
Chapman's
Baobab
133
Tsoe
Ntwetwe Pan
Sukwane
3
Rakops
21° 0' 57" S
24° 21' 42" E
Dzibui
Pan
Guguago
Pan
Nkokwane
Pan
Tsokotsa
Pan
View of
Sua Pan
Xhumo
Mmatshumo

Index

Index

Index

Resources

NAMIBIAN CONTACT DETAILS & INFORMATION

Namibia (country code 00264)

Namibian Tourism Board
Tel: 061 290 6000
Fax: 061 254 848
www.namibiatourism.com.na

Namibia Wildlife Resorts Central Reservations Office
Tel: 061 285 7200
Fax: 061 224 900
reservations@nwr.com.na
www.nwr.com.na

NWR Swakopmund Office
Tel: 064 402 172
Fax: 064 402 796
sw.bookings@nwr.com.na

NWR Cape Town Office
Tel: +27 21 4223761
Fax: +27 21 4225148
ct.bookings@nwr.com.na

The Cardboard Box Travel Shop
Tel: 061 256 580
Fax: 061 256 581
info@namibian.org
www.namibian.org

Police
The national emergency number for the Police is 10111.

Telephone enquiries
For numbers that have changed or are not listed in the telephone directory, dial 1188.
www.namdirectory.com

State Hospitals
Tel: 061 203 9111

Gobabis (062)
Municipality
Tel: 56 2551
Fax: 56 3012
ceogomun@iafrica.com.na
www.gobmun.com

Gobabis Tourism Info
Tel: 56 4743
Fax: 56 4169
contact@gobabis.net
www.gobabis.net

Uaki Wilderness Tourist Info
Tel: 56 4743
Fax: 56 4169
www.uakii.com

Grootfontein (067)
Grootfontein Municipal & Tourism Office
Tel: 243 100
Fax: 242 930
www.grootfonteinmun.com.na

Henties Bay (064)
Tourist Office
Tel: 50 1143
Fax: 50 1142

Henties Bay Tourism Association
info@hentiesbaytourism.com
www.hentiesbaytourism.com

Municipality
Tel: 50 2000
Fax: 50 2001
www.hentiesbay.org

Katima Mulilo(066)
Tourist Office
Tutwa Tourism and Travel
Tel/Fax: 25 2739/3048
www.tutwa.com

Municipality
Tel: 25 3586/3003
Fax: 25 3212

Keetmanshoop (063)
Ministry of Environment & Tourism
Tel: 22 3223
Fax: 22 5629

Southern Tourist Forum
Tel: 22 1266/11
Fax: 22 3813/8

Municipality
Tel: 22 1212
Fax: 22 3818
ceo@keetmanshoop-municipality.org.na
www.keetmansmunicipality.org.na

Lüderitz (063)
Lüderitz Town Council
Tel: 20 2041
Fax: 20 2971

Okahandja (062)
Gross Barmen Hot Springs Resort
Tel: 50 1091
Fax: 50 1094

Municipality
Tel: 50 5100
Fax: 50 1746
www.okahandja.org.na

Omaruru (064)
Omaruru Game Lodge
Tel: 57 0044
Fax: 57 0134
omlodge@iafrica.com.za

Ministry of Environment and Tourism – Tourist Info
Tel: 57 1194
Fax: 57 1195

Municipality
Tel: 57 0028
Fax: 57 0105

Resources

Opuwo (065)
Ministry of Environment & Tourism
Tel: 27 3003
Fax: 27 3171/52

The Kaoko Info Centre
Tel: 27 3420

Municipality
Tel: 27 3007/70
Fax: 27 3250/65

Oshakati (065)
Municipality
Tel: 22 9500
info@oshtc.na
www.oshtc.na

Otjiwarongo (067)
Tourist Office/Omaue Information
Tel/Fax: 30 3830/2231

Municipality
Tel: 30 2231
Fax: 30 2098
www.otjiwarongomun.org

Outjo (067)
Etosha Information Bureau
Tel/Fax: 31 3072

Etosha National Park (South Africa)
Tel: +27 21 853 7952
Fax: +27 21 853 8391
www.etoshanationalpark.co.za

Municipality
Tel: 31 3013/113
Fax: 31 3065
outmun@mweb.com.na
www.outjomunicipality.com

Rehoboth (062)
Lake Oanob Resort
Tel: 061 256 580
Fax: 061 256 581

Town Council of Rehoboth
Tel: 52 2091
Fax: 52 2090

Rundu (066)
Ministry of Environment & Tourism
Tel: 25 5749
Fax: 25 5789
www.met.gov.na

Rundu Tourist Info
Tel: 25 6140

Municipality/Town Council
Tel: 26 6400
Fax: 25 6718/87

Sesfontein (065)
Fort Sesfontein Lodge & Safaris
Tel: 68 5034/32
Fax: 68 5033
info@fort-sesfontein.com
www.fort-sesfontein.com

Swakopmund (064)
Municipality of Swakopmund
Tel: 410 4111
Fax: 410 4121
swkmun@swkmun.com.na
www.swkmun.com.na

Tsumeb (067)
Travel North Guesthouse Namibia
Tel: 22 0728
Fax: 22 0916
info@travelnorthguesthouse.com
www.natron.net

Municipality
Tel: 22 1056
Fax: 22 1467/4
www.tsumeb.info

Walvis Bay (064)
Tourist Office
Tel: 20 9170
Fax: 20 9171
www.walvisbay.com.na

Municipality
Tel: 201 3111
Fax: 20 5590
www.walvisbaycc.org.na

Windhoek (061)
Information Office
Tel: 290 2092/2596
oft@windhoekcc.org.na
www.windhoekcc.org.na

Municipality
Tel: 290 2690

Car Hire
Comprehensive list of available car hire firms:
www.grnnet.gov.na

Airports managed by Namibia Airport Company (NAC)
- Hosea Kutako International Airport
- Keetmanshoop Airport
- Ondangwa Airport
- Rundu Airport
- Katima Mulilo Airport
- Eros Airport
- Walvis Bay Airport
- Lüderitz Airport

Resources

TOURIST INFORMATION

Entry Requirements

All visitors must have a valid passport, and temporary residence permits for visitors are issued on arrival and allow tourists a period of 90 days in the country. Bona fide tourists and business travellers from many countries are exempted from visa requirements. Visitors are, however, advised to confirm visa requirements with their travel agent.

Health Requirements

Vaccinations against smallpox, cholera and yellow fever are not required. However, visitors travelling from or through countries where yellow fever is endemic must have a valid International Certificate of Vaccination. This requirement does not apply to air travellers in transit. No AIDS screening tests are conducted.

Air Travel

Hosea Kutako International Airport, 45km (28 miles) west of the capital, is the major point of entry into Namibia. Eros Airport, 4km (2.5 miles) from the city centre, is served by domestic flights. Air Namibia, the national carrier, has regular scheduled flights to Katima Mulilo, Lüderitz, Ondangwa, Oranjemund, Rundu and Walvis Bay. There are landing strips throughout the country and air charter services are available in Windhoek, Swakopmund and Walvis Bay.

Road Travel

Namibia has a well-developed road system, covering some 45,400km (28,212 miles). Trunk roads covering 6400km (3977 miles) are tarred and connect all the main centres, while major gravel-surface roads are generally in a good condition. The state of district and farm roads varies from good to poor, depending on when they were last graded.
Motoring Tips: During the summer months care should be exercised on gravel-surface roads as washaways are common after rains. Motorists should look out for wild or domestic animals as they can cause serious accidents. Always carry emergency spares and sufficient water (at least 10 litres; 2.6 gallons), especially on the lonely back roads.
Driver's licence: The carrying of driver's licences is now compulsory. Foreign licences are acceptable if they carry a photograph and are either printed in English or accompanied by an English-language certificate of authenticity. An alternative is to obtain an International Driving Permit before departing for Namibia. Licences issued in Botswana, Lesotho, South Africa, Swaziland and Zimbabwe are valid in Namibia.
Road Rules And Signs: In Namibia one drives on the left-hand side of the road. The speed limit on major roads is 120kph (75mph) and in urban areas 60kph (37mph), unless otherwise indicated. Depending on the condition of gravel-surface roads, the recommended speed is between 80kph (50mph) and 100kph (62mph). All proclaimed routes are numbered and tourist attractions are generally well marked.
Petrol: Petrol is available at filling stations throughout Namibia. In Windhoek and some of the larger towns fuel is available 24 hours a day, but in some of the smaller towns and settlements pumps close at 18:00, while restricted hours could apply during weekends. The availability of fuel at some settlements in remote areas is unreliable at times and you should ensure that you have sufficient fuel to get to your destination. In the northwest of Namibia petrol is available only at Ruacana, Sesfontein and Opuwo. Cash only is accepted for petrol in rural areas.
Automobile Association of Namibia: The AAN office is in the Carl List Building, on the corner of Independence Avenue and Fidel Castro Street, tel: (061) 22 4201. The AA has tow-in service contractors in all major towns. The after-hours breakdown number is: (061) 22 4201.
Coach travel: Intercape Mainliner operates a luxury coach service between Windhoek and Walvis Bay, and between Windhoek and Victoria Falls. There are also regular coach departures from the capital to Cape Town and Johannesburg.

Medical Services

It is advisable to take out medical insurance before your departure for Namibia. Windhoek has three private hospitals (the Roman Catholic Hospital in Werner List Street, Medi-Clinic in Eros-park and the Rhino Park Private Hospital), there is a Medi-Clinic in Otjiwarongo and Swakopmund. Walvis Bay has the Welwitschia Hospital. Some churches in the north of the country run hospitals or clinics, and there are state hospitals in major towns. Membership of International SOS, a company which specialises in dealing with medical emergencies countrywide, is highly advisable, tel: (061) 289 0999, fax: 231 254.

Information courtesy of the Globetrotter Guide to Namibia by Willie Olivier, published by New Holland Publishers.